Kindle Fire

SCOTT McNULTY

Visual QuickStart Guide
Kindle Fire
Scott McNulty

Peachpit Press
1301 Sansome Street
San Francisco, CA 94111
415/675-5100
415/675-5157 (fax)

Find us on the Web at www.peachpit.com
To report errors, please send a note to errata@peachpit.com.
Peachpit Press is a division of Pearson Education.

Editor: Cliff Colby
Development editor: Kim Wimpsett
Production editor: Danielle Foster
Compositor: Danielle Foster
Copyeditor: Valerie Perry
Indexer: Valerie Perry
Cover Design: RHDG / Riezebos Holzbaur Design Group, Peachpit Press
Interior Design: Peachpit Press
Logo Design: MINE™ www.minesf.com

ISBN-13: 978-0-321-90387-7
ISBN-10:   0-321-90387-0

9 8 7 6 5 4 3 2 1

Printed and bound in the United States of America

Dedication

For Marisa, who doesn't mind that Kindles outnumber us 7 to 1.

Acknowledgments

Though my name is on the cover of this book, it is far from my effort alone. My sincere thanks to everyone at Peachpit who worked on a very tight deadline to make this book as good as it is. Cliff Colby continues to believe in my writing and puts up with my frantic e-mails. Kim Wimpsett once again took the clay of my words and shaped them into something worth reading—my thanks for that. My thanks also to Danielle Foster for managing the production of the book and for doing the layout and to Valerie Perry for the copyediting and indexing.

Any mistakes are my own.

Contents at a Glance

Table of Contents

Meet your Kindle Fire

Amazon would have you believe that anyone can pick up a Kindle Fire and start using it without having any trouble. While the Kindle Fire is amazingly easy to use, given how powerful it is, many aspects of the device aren't evident right out of the box. (You'll notice that the box contains precious little physical documentation to help you get started.)

This chapter introduces the basics of your Kindle Fire so you can start using it like a pro in no time at all.

In this chapter

Hardware and specifications

Amazon sells four different models of the Kindle Fire: three Kindle Fire HD models and one model simply called Kindle Fire. The three Kindle Fire HD models all share the same basic physical controls and ports (**A** and **B**), while the Kindle Fire lacks a camera and physical volume buttons.

The HD models sport an improved screen capable of displaying high-definition (HD) video.

Status bar

Camera

Display

Carousel

Related content

A The front of the 7-inch Kindle Fire HD

Storage and the cloud

Every Kindle Fire model has a certain amount of on-device storage. You can use this storage for movies, TV shows, books, pictures, music, and apps. In addition to the storage on the device, Amazon stores all of the content that you purchase from Amazon on its *cloud*, or its servers. The great thing is Amazon holds onto the content for you and you can access it using your Kindle Fire without taking up any of your local storage. A network connection is required to access any content on the cloud. Anything stored on the device itself can be accessed with or without an Internet connection.

The Kindle Fire is the cheapest model and doesn't include a front-facing camera or support HD video. The other Kindle Fires (the 7-inch and two 8.9-inch versions) have HD screens. For a complete list of specifications and to compare the different models to one another, visit www.amazon.com/kindle/.

TIP No matter which Kindle Fire you have, it is running the same operating system: Google's Android 4.0 (also known as Ice Cream Sandwich). If you've used another Android tablet or smartphone, you might be surprised because the Fire looks nothing like them. Amazon created a custom look, or user interface, for Google's mobile operating system.

Included in the box with each Kindle Fire is a *Quick Start Guide* plus a USB 2.0 cable for charging and transferring data from your computer. A wall power charger is not included, though Amazon sells one for $19.99 (or $9.99 when you purchase one at the same time as your Kindle Fire).

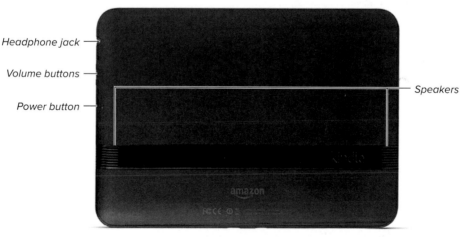

Headphone jack
Volume buttons
Power button
Speakers

B The back of the 7-inch Kindle Fire HD

Locking and powering on and off

Your Kindle Fire's Power button serves double duty. It allows you to turn on and off the device; also, pressing it puts your Kindle Fire to sleep and locks the screen. A sleeping Kindle Fire uses much less power. However, it will continue to play music (though movies and TV shows will be paused automatically), and the volume buttons continue to work. The Kindle Fire will also check periodically for new notifications from your various apps including new e-mails, calendar reminders, and other things you might want to know about. If you have an alert sound assigned to notifications, that sound will play even if your Kindle Fire is sleeping. (See the "Working with notifications" section, later in this chapter, for more information.)

When your Kindle Fire is sleeping/locked, you can interact only with the Lock screen, which on many models of Kindle Fire displays special offers (see Chapter 15 for more information).

A powered-off Kindle Fire is completely shut down. The device isn't connected to any wireless networks, and notifications aren't updated. The battery still drains slowly, but eventually, even a powered-off Kindle Fire will run out of battery power.

To put your Kindle Fire to sleep:

- Press the Power button on your Kindle Fire Ⓐ.

Power button

Ⓐ The Kindle Fire HD Power button

Amazon leather case lets you enjoy your content hands-free

Shop now

B The Lock screen. Slide to unlock.

Do you want to shut down your Kindle?

Cancel   Shut Down

C Tap Shut Down to turn off your Kindle Fire.

To wake your Kindle Fire:

- Press the Power button, and the Lock screen is displayed **B**. To unlock, simply press your finger against the icon and slide it to the left.

To power off your Kindle Fire:

1. Press and hold the Power button until the Shut Down message appears **C**.
2. Tap Shut Down.

To power on your Kindle Fire:

1. Press the Power button.
2. Wait a few moments as the device boots up and shows the Lock screen.

TIP To set the screen *timeout*, which is the delay before your Kindle Fire automatically goes to sleep and locks itself, swipe down from the top of the device and tap More > Sounds & Display > Screen Timeout.

Charging

The two ways to charge your Kindle Fire both involve the micro-USB port on the bottom edge of the device next to the mini-HDMI port **A**. The current battery level is displayed at the top right of every screen on the Kindle Fire **B**. As the battery drains, the icon is filled in less and less. When the battery dips below 20 percent, the icon turns red to indicate that you should charge your Kindle Fire soon.

You can either plug your Kindle Fire into a computer to charge it or use a micro-USB power adapter to charge directly from a power outlet.

To charge via computer:

1. Plug the included micro-USB cable into your Kindle Fire and insert the other end into either a Mac or a PC with a powered USB port.

2. The battery icon turns green and pulses to indicate that it is charging **C**.

3. The Kindle Fire will charge fully in about 11.5 hours from 0 percent battery.

TIP If you plug your Fire into an underpowered USB port, the battery icon won't turn green. An alert will also appear letting you know that the Fire will charge slowly, and only while asleep **D**.

To charge via a micro-USB adapter:

TIP You must have a micro-USB adapter handy to charge using this method. Amazon sells one especially for the Kindle Fire **E**.

1. Plug the USB cable into the micro-USB port on the Kindle Fire and insert the power adapter into an outlet.

2. The battery icon will turn green to indicate that the Fire is charging.

3. The Kindle Fire will charge fully via this method in about 4 hours (3.5 if you're using Amazon's official Power-Fast charger).

A The micro-USB and mini-HDMI ports on the Kindle Fire HD

B The battery icon gives you a sense of how much power your Kindle Fire has left. This Fire has a little less than half of its battery remaining.

C When your Kindle Fire is charging, the battery icon pulses green.

Connected to Low-Power Charger
Your Kindle may not charge while in use. If you leave it connected, it will charge slowly while the device is asleep.

D Plugging your Kindle Fire into a lower-power USB will charge it eventually, as this alert points out.

E The Amazon PowerFast charger

Welcome to Kindle Fire
Connect to a Wi-Fi Network

Apt 2024 FiOS
Secured with WPA/WPA2 PSK

NETGEAR48
Secured with WPA/WPA2 PSK

1919chest1822
Secured with WPA/WPA2 PSK

Complete setup later

A Tap the Wi-Fi network in order to connect your Fire to it.

Register Your Kindle

Enter Amazon Account Info

E-mail address

smcnulty@gmail.com

Password

••••••••••••••••

✓ Hide Password

Register

By registering or creating an account, you agree to all the terms found here.

New to Amazon?

Create Account

← Back

B Enter your Amazon account information. If you don't have an Amazon account, create one by tapping Create Account.

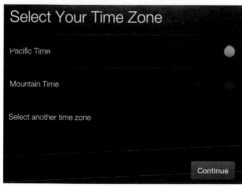

Select Your Time Zone

Pacific Time

Mountain Time

Select another time zone

Continue

C Select your time zone.

Setting up

The true power of the Kindle Fire comes from the tight integration with Amazon services. If you purchased your Kindle Fire directly from Amazon, not as a gift, then it will be preregistered to your Amazon account. You can reset your Kindle Fire to factory defaults at any time; this erases all content on the device and deregisters it from your Amazon account. When you turn it on, It'll walk you through the setup process.

This task assumes that your Kindle Fire is not preregistered to an Amazon account. If yours is, you can skip the parts regarding registering the Kindle Fire.

To turn on your Kindle Fire for the first time:

1. Turn on your Kindle Fire by pressing the Power button at the top of the device. It is located next to the headphone jack.

2. The Kindle Fire will boot up and search for available Wi-Fi networks **A**. Tap your Wi-Fi network of choice and enter a user name and password if prompted.

3. Enter the e-mail address and password for the Amazon account you want to register this Kindle Fire with **B**. If you don't have an Amazon account, you can create one by tapping the Create Account button and entering the information requested.

TIP Make sure to enable Hide Password if you're setting up your Kindle Fire in public. You don't want people to see your Amazon password.

4. Tap your time zone and then tap Continue **C**.

continues on next page

5. Confirm that this is the Amazon account you want to register your Kindle Fire with by tapping Continue 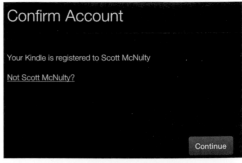. If this isn't the account information you were expecting, tap the Not Scott McNulty link (your link will display your name).

6. Connect your Facebook and Twitter accounts if you want to share content from your Kindle Fire with your social networks ⓔ. Tap either account and then enter your user name and password. Tap Connect to associate that social networking account with your Amazon account.

TIP **If you have previously associated a Twitter or Facebook account with your Amazon account, it will be set automatically.**

7. Tap Get Started Now. A brief tutorial is shown, giving you a good overview of your Kindle Fire's functionality ⓕ.

8. Now your Kindle Fire is ready to be used. Your Kindle books and documents are displayed in the Carousel. If you have any music on Amazon's cloud, you'll be able to access it immediately.

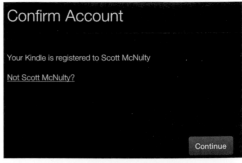

ⓓ Tap Continue if this is the Amazon account you want to use for registering your Fire.

ⓔ You can link some of your social media accounts to your Kindle Fire.

ⓕ The tutorial shows you some basic information about the Fire.

Using gestures

The Kindle Fire is driven almost entirely by touch. If you want to launch an app, interact with content, or do just about anything with your Fire, you just touch it in a variety of ways.

The Kindle Fire is a *multitouch* device, which means it is more advanced than touchscreens of old. It can recognize more gestures and allows you to use multiple fingers to achieve them. The Kindle Fire has *two-point multitouch support*, meaning it can track and respond to two touches at once while the Kindle Fire HDs all support up to ten points.

Table 1.1 explains the touch nomenclature that will be used throughout this book, and across multitouch devices in general.

TABLE 1.1 Touch Terminology

Command	Action
Tap	Press your finger against the screen and release quickly.
Long tap	Press your finger against an icon on the screen and hold it there for a moment. This will usually bring up additional options.
Double tap	Tap the screen twice.
Swipe	Press your finger against the screen. Move your finger down, up, left, or right and then release. You'll use this often because this is the command that unlocks your Kindle Fire.
Drag	Long tap an item and then, still pressing your finger against the screen, move your finger. This is used to move icons and select text, among other things.
Pinch	This is just like pinching a cheek, only you're pinching against a slab of glass. Spread two fingers apart or together while pressed against the screen. This is used to zoom in on pictures. Separating your fingers zooms out, while bringing them together zooms in.

Using basic navigation

The Kindle Fire's Home screen isn't where you'll spend most of your time when using the device, but it is a very important part of the experience. The Home screen is a central location that gives you access to everything on your Fire with a couple of taps. The Home screen is divided into five different sections: the status bar, Search, library navigation, the Carousel, and the Related section .

When viewed in landscape mode, the Home screen becomes simplified **B**. The Search box and the Related section are hidden, and more of the Carousel is displayed. Just tilt the device to switch from landscape to portrait if you want access to the Search box and the Related section at any time.

Once you've hopped into a section of your Kindle Fire, you'll want to know how to get back to your Home screen. In-app navigation is generally straightforward with a couple of caveats.

> **TIP** Tapping the star on the lower-right corner of the Home screen will bring up your Favorites (see the "Working with Favorites" section for more information).

To use the Home screen:

- The status bar displays relevant data about your Kindle Fire: the device's name (Scott's 12th Kindle **A**), the number of active notifications (if any), the time, your wireless connections and their strength, and the battery level. The status bar is also displayed in many apps, though some apps fade it out after a bit (like when you're reading a book or watching a movie) so that the full screen displays your content and nothing else.

A The Home screen in portrait mode

B The landscape version of the Home screen. Notice that the Search box and Related section aren't shown.

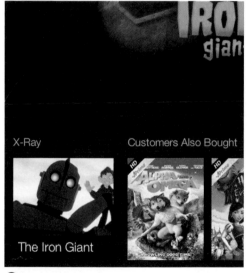

C When a piece of media purchased from Amazon has focus on the Carousel, the Related content consists of things that you might like to buy based on the focused item.

D This button is displayed when the X-Ray feature is available on a movie or book.

- The Search box is visible only on the Home screen when you're holding the Kindle Fire in portrait mode. Tapping in the Search box will allow you to search across your device.

- All of your Kindle Fire content is stored in a number of libraries, including Games, Apps, and Music. The library navigation lists all of the available libraries. Swipe left and right to scroll through them, and then tap the library you want to be taken to.

- The Carousel displays any content that you've recently accessed: launched or newly installed apps, books you're currently reading, the last website you visited, the music you're currently listening to, and any videos you recently watched. The items are arranged in chronological order with the most recently accessed displayed first. Swipe left and right to look through the Carousel. Tap any of the icons to use the app or consume the content it represents.

- The Related section displays a variety of things when you're looking at the Home screen in portrait mode, depending on the content that is in focus. As you swipe along the Carousel, the item in the center of the screen has focus. While a video, book, audiobook, or app purchased from Amazon is in focus, the Related section displays what customers who purchased that item also bought **C**. If you tap one of the recommendations, you'll be taken to that item's entry in the appropriate Amazon store where you can purchase and download it.

   If a book or movie supports X-Ray, a button taking you right the X-Ray section is displayed for your tapping **D**.

continues on next page

The built-in E-mail, Calendar, and Contacts apps display as three special Quick Links in the Related section when they're in focus: New Message, This Week, and Favorite Contacts **E**.

Finally, when a Web page is in focus, Trending Now is displayed in the Related section **F**. These are websites that lots of Kindle Fire users are visiting. Swipe left and right to see them all, and tap to visit one.

TIP If your Kindle Fire has Special Offers enabled (more on this in Chapter 15), text ads will be displayed from time to time in the bottom-left corner of the Home screen. Tap the ad if you're interested in learning more.

To remove items from the Carousel:

1. Recently accessed content is automatically added to your Carousel to make switching between things easy, but sometimes you don't want an item in your Carousel. Long tap the item you want to remove.

2. Tap Remove from Carousel to remove the item **G**. It is still on your Fire, just not displayed on the Carousel (if you want to remove it completely, tap Remove from Device).

TIP Add things to your Favorites right from the Carousel by long tapping and tapping Add to Favorites.

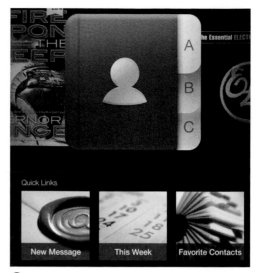

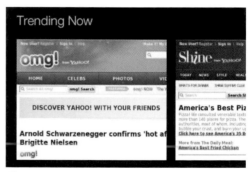

E E-mail, Calendar, and Contacts all display the same three quick links when they are in focus on the Carousel.

F Trending sites are displayed when your most recently visited website is in focus.

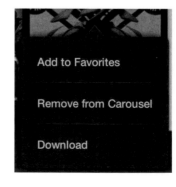

G Long tap and tap Remove from Carousel if you don't want something showing up.

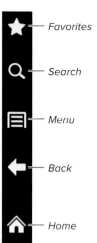

Favorites

Search

Menu

Back

Home

H The Favorites button (the star), the Back button (the arrow), and the Home button (the house) are all mainstays on the in-app navigation bar.

To navigate in apps:

- Apps, and each library, all have different functions. As a result, navigating within them varies. However, regardless of what you're doing on your Kindle Fire when you're away from the Home screen, a navigation bar is displayed either at the bottom of the screen (when in portrait mode) or on the right edge (in landscape) **H**.

- The navigation bar might include context-specific icons, but it will always show two icons: the Home button and the Favorites star.

- Tap the Home button to return to the Home screen, and tap the star to browse your Favorites.

- The Back button is often, but not always, present as well **H**. Tapping this button will return you to the screen you were on just before tapping it. When you launch an app from the Home screen, for example, and then tap the Back button, you'll be returned to the Home screen because that's where you were precisely before launching the app. If you are in the Music library and you select an artist from the artist list and then tap Back, you'll return to the full artist list. Tapping the Back button repeatedly will step you through all the screens you navigated to get to your current location.

TIP Some apps hide the navigation bar so they can display content full screen. Tap the screen, and a small handle will appear where the navigation bar is normally located. Tap the handle to access the navigation bar.

Working with Favorites

Unlike some other tablets, the Kindle Fire doesn't offer what's known as an *application switcher*. An application switcher allows you to change quickly from one application to another by using a special shortcut. However, you don't have to go back to the Home screen every time you want to switch to another app or piece of content. You can add frequently used apps, videos, songs, or books to a special area called *Favorites*. This gives you one-tap access to your favorites no matter where you are in the Kindle Fire interface.

To access Favorites:

- On the Home screen, tap the white star icon on the lower-right side of the screen. This will reveal the Favorites area .

- When you're not on the Home screen, the Favorites star icon appears on the navigation bar located on one edge of the screen; which edge it is on varies from section to section.

- Tapping one of your favorites takes you to that website, app, or piece of content. If you decide you don't actually want to go to one of your favorites, just swipe down, and the Favorites area closes.

A The Favorites feature gathers your most used apps/content, as defined by you, into one easy-to-access place.

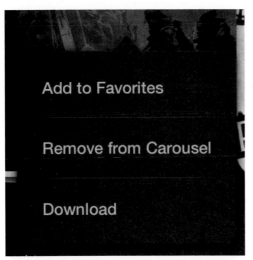

B Long tap anything in the Carousel and tap Add to Favorites to add the item to your favorites.

C Long tap a favorite and select Remove from Favorites to delete it from Favorites (the content is still on your Fire).

To add something to Favorites:

1. Long tap an item in the Carousel or in a library.
2. Tap Add to Favorites **B**.
3. The icon now appears in your Favorites.

To remove a favorite:

1. Long tap the favorite you want to remove.
2. Tap Remove from Favorites **C**.

TIP Your Kindle Fire knows what you have listed in your Favorites, so when you long tap something that is in your Favorites, the Remove from Favorites option appears no matter if you're tapping it in the Favorites, the Carousel, or its media library.

To rearrange your favorites:

1. Tap the Favorites star to open your favorites.
2. Tap and hold an icon that you want to move.
3. While holding onto the icon, slide your finger into the position where you want to move the icon.
4. Lift up your finger, and the icon will drop into its new position, moving aside any other favorites.

Working with notifications

Your Kindle Fire will alert you when certain things happen: a new e-mail arrives, a calendar event is coming up soon, and more. A sound will play, the number of notifications is displayed, and a message is added to the notifications area.

To view notifications:

1. The number of current notifications is displayed in the upper-left corner of the Home screen Ⓐ.

2. Swipe down from the top of the screen to see your current notifications Ⓑ.

3. Tapping a notification will take you to the app that generated it so you can take an action.

To remove notifications:

- As notifications pile up, you'll want to get rid of them. You can remove all of the notifications by tapping the Remove All button.

- Swipe across a notification to remove it selectively.

To turn off an application's notifications:

1. Notifications can be disabled per app by going to Quick Settings > More > Applications > Notification Settings Ⓒ.

2. Tap Off to turn off notifications for that app. You will no longer be notified for anything related to that app.

To set the notification sound:

1. You can set the sound notifications make by going to Quick Settings > More > Sounds & Displays > Notifications Sounds.

2. Tap the sound to preview it and set it as the notification sound. Tap another sound to switch.

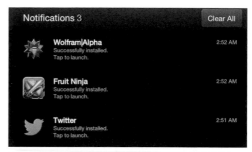

Ⓐ The number of current notifications is displayed in the upper-left corner of the screen.

Ⓑ All of your active notifications are displayed in the notifications area. Tap one to open the app that generated it.

Ⓒ Notifications can be toggled on and off per application.

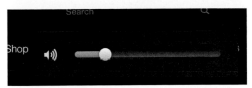

A The Volume slider in Quick Settings

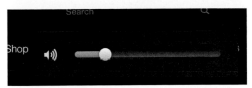

B When you use the physical Volume buttons, this on-screen Volume slider appears.

Changing the volume

The Kindle Fire HDs all include Dolby speakers that pump out a surprising amount of volume for a tablet. The Kindle Fire includes speakers, but they aren't as good as those on the HD models. The Kindle Fire also lacks physical buttons, but you can still control the volume.

To adjust the volume using settings:

1. On any Kindle Fire model, swipe down from the top to reveal the Settings menu.

2. Tap the Volume icon and slide your finger up and down on the Volume slider to increase or decrease the volume **A**. Slide all the way down to mute the device.

To use the Kindle Fire HD's physical buttons:

1. Locate the buttons above the Power button. This pair of buttons controls the volume.

2. The top button (located directly below the headphone jack) always increases the volume, and the lower button decreases the volume.

   Whenever you press either button, an on-screen volume indicator appears **B**. You can use this by tapping and sliding with your finger for more fine-grained volume control.

TIP Some applications include their own volume controls that impact the volume only within that app. The controls described here impact the volume level across the device.

Changing the brightness

The Kindle Fire's screen is capable of getting very bright, perhaps too bright. The brightness is easily adjustable, and you can even have the Kindle Fire auto-adjust the brightness depending on the ambient light in the room. When the Fire senses it is in a very bright room, it can automatically increase the screen's brightness, and vice versa, when it is in a dark room.

The brighter the screen, the faster your Kindle Fire will burn through a battery charge, so keep that in mind as you use it.

A The Automatic Brightness slider allows you to increase and decrease your Fire's screen brightness.

B Automatic Brightness uses a sensor to adjust the brightness of the screen without your input.

To manually adjust screen brightness:

1. Swipe down from the top of the Fire to access Quick Settings.

2. Tap the Brightness icon **A**.

3. By default, Automatic Brightness is disabled, so slide your finger along the Brightness control to increase or decrease the brightness. The screen brightness will change in real time.

4. Tap the Back button when you're happy with the brightness.

To enable automatic brightness:

1. Go to Quick Settings > Brightness.

2. Tap the On button next to Automatic Brightness.

3. The Brightness slider disappears, and now your Kindle Fire is managing the screen brightness for you **B**.

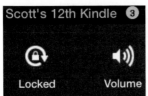

A The Orientation lock makes sure your Kindle Fire's screen orientation won't change from portrait to landscape.

Setting the orientation

The Kindle Fire has an accelerometer built into it that tells the device how you're holding it. When you're holding it in *portrait mode* (the narrow edge toward the bottom) the screen automatically rotates to display content correctly. Flip the Fire on its side into *landscape mode*, and once again, the screen automatically orients itself so you can keep on viewing content.

Generally, this is how you want your Kindle Fire to act, but sometimes you want to ensure that the screen won't rotate automatically while you're reading a book (as an example). That's why you can lock the screen in either portrait or landscape mode so the screen won't budge.

To lock orientation:

1. Hold the Kindle Fire with the screen oriented in the way you want to lock it.
2. Swipe down from the top of the screen to bring up Quick Settings.
3. Tap the Unlocked icon. It will switch to Locked **A**.
4. Move your Kindle Fire, and the screen will not automatically orient itself.

To unlock orientation:

1. Swipe down to bring up Quick Settings.
2. Tap the Locked Icon to unlock the screen. Now it will move freely.

TIP Some apps work only in landscape or portrait mode and will be presented in that mode regardless of the locked orientation.

Using the keyboard

Whenever you need to enter text on your Kindle Fire, an onscreen keyboard appears, as if by magic . The basic premise of a software keyboard is just like that of its hardware counterpart: Tap the letters you want to type and they appear. The laws of physics, however, don't limit a software keyboard. So, it can do some interesting things. For example, it can show a particular layout appropriate for the task at hand or try to guess what you're typing to save you a few taps.

A The Kindle Fire's onscreen keyboard

To type alternate characters:

1. Some keys on the keyboard are able to type more than one character. Bring up the keyboard and look at the letter e. Notice it has a small *3* in the upper-right corner.

2. Long tap the letter e, and a list of alternate characters that you can type appears **B**. If you simply lift your finger, the number 3 will be typed. Slide your finger over the alternate character that you would like to type if you don't want the default selection (highlighted in orange).

3. Tap any of the alternates to type that character.

B Long tap keys to display any alternate characters that are available.

TIP Experiment by long tapping keyboard characters to see whether they have alternate characters available.

C The number keyboard

D The symbol keyboard

| Brilli | **Brilliant** ... | Brilliantly |

E As you type, the Fire tries to guess what you want to say. Hit the spacebar to insert the word in the center, or tap one of the other suggestions.

Smatr

Share

Short

Smart

Shore

Shirt

+ Add to Dictionary

✕ Delete

F Spell check suggestions

To view numbers and symbols:

1. Tap the ?123 key to switch to the number keyboard **C**.

2. Tap =\< while on the number keyboard to get the symbol keyboard **D**.

To implement suggestions:

1. As you're typing, you'll notice that a list of suggestions appears at the top of the keyboard **E**.

2. The middle suggestion is the Kindle's best guess. If you press the spacebar, it will insert that suggested word into whatever you're typing.

3. To use another one of the suggestions, just tap it, and it is inserted. Continue typing to ignore all the suggestions.

To use spell check:

1. As you type, unrecognized words are underlined in red.

2. Tap the word, and a list of suggestions appears **F**.

3. If you would rather use one of the suggested spellings, tap it. You can also add the word to your Fire's custom dictionary by tapping +Add to Dictionary, and it will no longer be underlined. If you want to get rid of the word altogether, tap Delete.

To customize the keyboard:

1. Long tap the Comma button, and the Keyboard Settings button appears **G**.

2. Tap it and then tap Keyboard in the Input Options window.

3. Now you can change a number of keyboard settings by tapping the appropriate setting **H**.

TIP You can also get to the keyboard settings when the keyboard isn't onscreen via Quick Settings > More > Keyboard.

G The Keyboard Preferences key

Keyboard

Auto-Capitalization	**On**	Off
Sound on Keypress	On	**Off**
Auto Correction		
Space bar and punctuation automatically correct mistyped words		
Show Correction Suggestions		
Always show		
Spelling Suggestions	**On**	Off
Highlight misspelled words in text fields		

H Keyboard preferences give you control over how you input text.

2

Wireless

The Kindle Fire is a window into your Amazon world, which is dependent on network access. All Kindle Fire models support Wi-Fi connectivity, so you can easily connect to your home wireless network and a wide variety of public networks. The HD models also offer Bluetooth connectivity for a large number of peripherals. This chapter covers how to connect with each of these wireless options and how to disable them all when the need arises.

In this chapter

Hooking up to Wi-Fi

Wi-Fi networks are seemingly everywhere these days. From your home to your office and even when you're traveling, wireless Internet usually isn't too far away. Your Kindle Fire is most useful when it is connected to the Internet, and it offers a number of Wi-Fi settings to make this possible.

No matter how you connect to a Wi-Fi network, your Kindle Fire will display this icon in the status bar: 🛜. This icon means you're connected to a Wi-Fi network, and the number of arcs relates to the strength of your connection: the more arcs shown, the better your connection.

To turn Wi-Fi on or off:

1. Swipe down and tap Wireless on Quick Settings **A**.

2. Tap Off in the Wi-Fi section to turn off Wi-Fi only (Bluetooth and LTE, if available on your Kindle Fire, will remain active).

3. Tap On to turn it back on.

To join an open Wi-Fi network:

1. Swipe down and tap Wireless on Quick Settings.

2. Make sure Wi-Fi is On.

3. The list of available Wi-Fi networks is displayed under Connect to a Network. Networks displayed with a lock require a user name/password.

4. Tap the open network (without a Lock icon) you want to join.

   The Kindle Fire connects. The Wi-Fi icon next to the network name turns orange and gets a check mark **B**.

5. Enjoy the Internet.

A The Wi-Fi settings are grouped together with the other wireless options on your Fire.

B When you're connected to a network, the Wi-Fi symbol turns orange and displays a check mark.

C A password is required to join encrypted networks. Your Fire will remember both the network and the password.

D If your network doesn't broadcast its SSID (or name), you can still add it manually. You need to know the name and type of security it uses, if any.

To join a password-protected network:

1. Swipe down and tap Wireless.

2. From the list of Wi-Fi networks, tap the encrypted, or password-protected, network you want to join (denoted by a Lock icon).

3. Enter the user name/password when prompted **C**.

4. Tap Connect.

> **TIP** Your Kindle Fire remembers all the networks you've connected to. When you're back in range of a remembered network, it will automatically reconnect. There's no need to enter a user name/password; the Kindle Fire remembers those as well.

To add a Wi-Fi network:

1. If the network you want to join isn't listed under Connect to a Network, you'll have to add it manually by tapping Add Network.

2. Enter the network's name, or service set ID (SSID), and select the type of security, if any, used by this network. If the network security requires a password, enter that as well **D**.

3. If you need to assign a static IP address to your Kindle Fire, tap the box next to "Show advanced options" and select Static from IP Settings. Enter the IP address information (if required).

4. Tap Save.

   The network is now listed, and you can connect to it by tapping it.

To forget a Wi-Fi network:

1. Long tap a network you've connected to previously.

2. Tap Forget .

   The network is no longer remembered by your Kindle Fire and will not be joined automatically when in range.

To find your Kindle Fire's MAC address:

1. Some networks use a unique number assigned to devices, called a Media Access Control (MAC) address, to decide who can join them. Swipe down to get to Quick Settings and tap More.

2. Tap Device > About.

   The Wi-Fi MAC address is displayed onscreen .

To get information about your wireless connection:

1. Open the Wireless settings (swipe down and tap Wireless).

2. Tap the network you're currently connected to (the Wi-Fi icon will be orange with a check mark).

   An information alert is displayed with your current IP address, signal strength, and more .

E Tapping the wireless network you're connected to gives you some information about the connection: signal strength, speed, and even your Fire's assigned IP address.

F Your Fire's unique MAC address is displayed on the About device screen. The MAC address in this image has been blurred out.

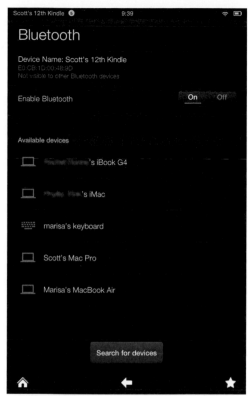

Hooking up to Bluetooth

Bluetooth is a short-range wireless standard that connects your tablet or computer to peripherals without messy wires. You're probably familiar with Bluetooth headsets that some people use with their phones so they can talk hands-free. This same technology is built into your Kindle Fire HD (and you can pair that headset to your Fire, if you like).

TIP Only the Kindle Fire HD models are equipped with Bluetooth.

To enable Bluetooth:

1. Swipe down to bring up Quick Settings and then tap Wireless.

2. Tap Bluetooth.

3. Tap On in the Enable Bluetooth section **A**.

   A grayed-out Bluetooth icon appears in the status bar denoting that Bluetooth is on but no Bluetooth devices are connected or paired **B**.

A All the Bluetooth settings and nearby devices (paired and not) are displayed on the Bluetooth settings screen.

B The Bluetooth icon is displayed in the status bar when Bluetooth is enabled.

To connect Bluetooth peripherals:

1. With Bluetooth enabled, go to Quick Settings > Wireless > Bluetooth.

2. A list of nearby Bluetooth devices will shortly appear under "Available devices."

3. If the device you want is on the list, tap it; if not, tap the "Search for devices" button to rescan the area.

4. When you tap the device you want to pair, instructions will appear 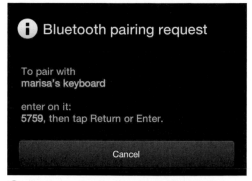.

5. Follow the instructions. Here, the pairing involves a keyboard, so the numbers displayed must be entered on the keyboard to confirm the pairing.

6. After a successful pairing, the device is listed in the Paired section 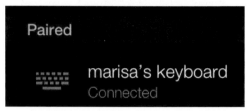.

   You can now use the Bluetooth device with your Kindle Fire.

To manage paired devices:

1. Go to Quick Settings > Wireless > Bluetooth.

2. Long tap the paired device you want to manage .

3. If you no longer want this device paired with your Fire, tap Unpair. If you want to rename the device that displays on your Fire, tap Rename and type in a new name.

C A pairing request from a keyboard

D Paired Bluetooth devices are grouped together.

E Long tapping a paired device allows you to unpair or rename it.

> **Device Name: Scott's 12th Kindle**
>
> Only visible to paired devices

F When Bluetooth is enabled, your Fire looks for other Bluetooth devices, but it doesn't broadcast its availability.

> **Device Name: Scott's 12th Kindle**
>
> Visible to all nearby Bluetooth devices (1:53)

G Tapping the device name in the Bluetooth settings makes your Fire "discoverable" by other Bluetooth-enabled devices, such as computers.

To make your Kindle Fire Bluetooth discoverable:

1. Bluetooth devices can be in either Discoverable mode or not. When in Discoverable mode, the device sends out a signal to other nearby devices advertising that it is pairable. By default, the Kindle Fire searches only for Bluetooth devices; it doesn't advertise itself. If you want to pair your computer with the Fire first, you must open the Bluetooth settings (Quick Settings > Wireless > Bluetooth).

2. At the top of the screen, your Bluetooth Device Name is displayed **F**. Under it is your Kindle Fire's Bluetooth ID text that reads "Only visible to paired devices." Tap the name.

3. The text changes to "Visible to all nearby Bluetooth devices" followed by a two-minute countdown **G**. For the next two minutes, your Kindle Fire is discoverable to any nearby devices that are searching.

TIP Tap the Bluetooth name any time during the two-minute countdown to stop the advertising.

Setting Airplane mode

If you've traveled on a plane in the past decade, you're familiar with the requirement that all portable devices must be turned off during take-off and landing. Furthermore, all wireless connectivity must be disabled on all devices for the duration of the flight.

Because the Kindle Fire is a great way to consume media on a plane, it makes sense that you'll be traveling with it. Airplane mode makes it simple to turn off all wireless on your device and still enjoy any content you've downloaded to it.

To enable Airplane mode:

1. Swipe down to access Quick Settings.

2. Tap Wireless.

3. Tap On next to Airplane Mode .

   All of your Fire's wireless options (Wi-Fi, Bluetooth, and LTE) are disabled, and a small airplane icon is displayed in the status bar **B**.

To disable Airplane mode:

1. Make sure your plane has landed and you're allowed to enable wireless.

2. Swipe down to bring up Quick Settings and then tap Wireless.

3. Tap Off next to Airplane Mode.

   The airplane icon in the status bar disappears, and your Kindle Fire is once again able to connect wirelessly.

TIP If you attempt to do something on your Kindle Fire that requires a network connection while Airplane mode is on, an alert will display **C**. Tap Wireless Settings if you want to connect anyway, or tap Cancel to go back to using your Kindle Fire in Airplane mode.

A The Airplane Mode toggle

B When Airplane mode is on, a small airplane icon appears in the status bar, replacing the Wi-Fi signal indicator.

Airplane Mode

A network connection is required to complete this task, and Airplane Mode automatically disables wireless connections. Please go to your wireless settings to turn off Airplane Mode or set up a Wi-Fi network.

Cancel   Wireless Settings

C You have no network connectivity with Airplane mode on, but you can still launch apps that attempt to use the network. In that case, your Fire alerts you and lets you jump to Wireless Settings.

3

Search

Search is a vital part of any device these days, and the Kindle Fire has a robust searching app that crosses content libraries, Amazon's stores, and the Web. You can access Unified Search, as it is known, in a variety of ways. You'll find having Unified Search at your fingertips particularly useful after you've been using your Fire for a while and have a large amount of content to sift through.

This chapter looks at each of the three main search varieties: libraries, stores, and Web.

In this chapter

Using libraries to search

All of the content on your Kindle Fire is organized into a number of libraries: music, books, personal documents, pictures, contacts, and your e-mail if you've set up an e-mail account. (Chapter 16 shows you how to do this.) You can easily search across all of those libraries by using Unified Search.

To get to the Unified Search app:

- While holding your Kindle Fire in portrait orientation, tap the Search box displayed on the Home screen **Ⓐ**.

- A Search icon appears on the Home screen library navigation bar. Swipe until you see the magnifying glass icon **🔍**. Tap it to enter Search **Ⓑ**.

To search your Kindle Fire libraries:

1. Open the Search app as described in the previous section.

2. Type in a query. The results update as you are typing.

Ⓐ The Search box on the Home screen appears only in portrait mode.

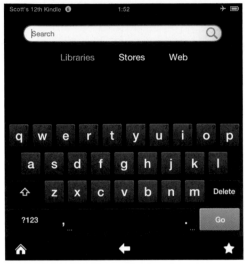

Ⓑ Search across all the content in your libraries at once.

C Search results are grouped by library and app. Tap any result to open it.

D If you tap a book in your cloud library, it starts to download to the device automatically.

3. Swipe up and down to scroll through the results **C**. Content from each library is grouped together in sections, including e-mail messages and contacts. Search results also include items stored in your cloud libraries (content you own but haven't downloaded to your Kindle Fire).

4. Tap the item you want to open from the search results. If you tap an item in the cloud, it is first downloaded to your Kindle Fire **D**. Tap again after downloading to open it.

TIP This method does not search through the text of books, periodicals, or documents—just the titles and authors. E-mail and contacts, on the other hand, have their text fully searched.

5. If your search query doesn't return any results, a "No library results" message displays **E**. Don't despair because you can run the same query again in the Amazon store or on the Web by tapping the appropriate links.

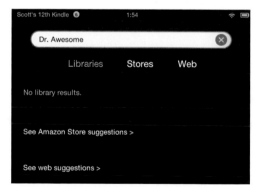

E When a search term isn't found in your libraries, you can tap either the Amazon store or Web suggestion links to perform the search in the store or across the Web.

Searching stores

Your Kindle Fire has access to a number of different Amazon stores, including the Kindle bookstore, music, and videos, and you can even purchase things from Amazon's physical inventory. The stores search looks across all the Amazon stores to find just the item you're looking for.

As you type, it suggests queries for specific stores 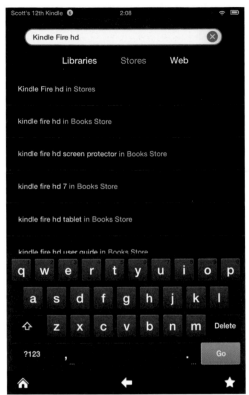.

To search stores:

1. Tap the Search icon in the library navigation or the Search box on the Home screen.

2. Tap Stores in the Search app to limit your searches to the stores.

3. Start typing your query.

4. The top suggested search will always be the exact phrase you typed into the Search box **A**. Tapping that suggestion will search across all the stores for that phrase. Underneath that suggestion are more focused ones limited to certain stores (such as the Books store or the Patio, Lawn & Garden store). The query terms in the suggestions are displayed in bold, white type, while the store to be searched is listed in plain, white type.

5. Tap the suggestion that is a closest match to what you're looking for, and you'll be whisked away to that store **B**.

> **TIP** When tapping some of the results, you'll be taken to the Amazon Shop app, covered in detail in Chapter 4.

6. Tap the Back button to return to the Stores search to look for other things.

A The stores search suggests both possible items and the store to search for them in.

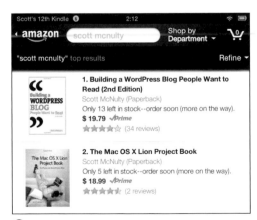

B A search for *Scott McNulty* across all of Amazon's stores

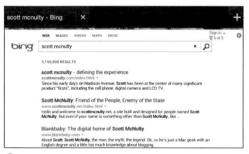

A The Web section of the Search app

B As you type, your search term suggestions appear. Tap the pencil to fill in the suggested term, or tap the term to execute a Web search using it.

C Your search terms are passed to Silk, which submits them to the search engine defined in settings (Bing by default).

Searching the Web

You can search the Web from your Kindle Fire in two ways: the Search app and via Silk, the Kindle Fire's Web browser. The Search app acts as a sort of broker for Web searches. When you tap a suggested search, it launches Silk, which performs the actual search using Bing—your default search engine.

To search the Web via the Search app:

1. Launch the Search app either by tapping the Search icon on the library navigation bar or by using the Search box on the Home screen.

2. Tap Web. It turns orange to indicate that you're performing a Web search **A**.

3. Start typing a query into the Search box. As you type, suggested searches are displayed **B**. Tap the pencil icon to paste the suggested query into the Search box (this can save you some typing with longer searches).

4. When you have entered your search terms, swipe up and down to scroll through all the suggestions.

5. Tap a suggestion to go to that search, or tap the Go button on the keyboard to search the exact phrase you entered.

6. Silk, the Fire's Web browser, is launched and displays your search **C**. Tap any of the links in the results that look interesting.

7. Tap the Back button to return to the Search app.

To search via the Web browser:

1. Open Silk by tapping Web in the library navigation on the Home screen.

2. If a Web page is already open, you need to open a new tab by tapping the + button .

3. Tap the URL field and type your search term **E**. As you type, a few things happen: Silk searches your browsing history and favorites and then suggests Web searches. The first suggested search is always for exactly what you typed (searches are denoted by a magnifying glass).

5. Tap the search you would like to perform, and you're taken to the results from the search engine of choice.

To change the default search engine:

1. By default, your Kindle Fire uses Microsoft Bing as its search engine. If that's not your thing, open Silk (tap Web on the library navigation on the Home screen) and then tap the menu icon on the navigation bar **F**.

2. Tap Settings. In the General section, you'll see which search engine is currently set as the default **G**.

3. Tap Search Engine to change your default search engine to Bing, Google, or Yahoo! **H**.

4. Now, when you perform a Web search, your chosen search engine will be used.

D The new tab button in Silk

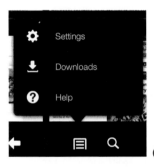

E Typing a search term in Silk's URL bar not only results in search suggestions but also searches your browsing history and bookmarks.

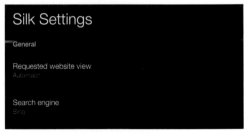

F The Silk menu

G Silk Settings with Bing set as the search engine

H The search engines that your Fire can use automatically

Shop

In addition to making the Kindle Fire, Amazon runs a little e-commerce website that sells everything from toothpicks to e-books. Of course, Amazon wants you to have access to the full Amazon shopping experience on your Kindle Fire, so it has created an app designed just for that.

Shopping is given its own place in the library navigation on the Home screen. The Shop app is an aggregator because it serves as a jumping-off point to the stores baked into the other libraries on the Kindle Fire (Books, Music, and Video). The Shop app is also a storefront because it lets you browse all the physical items for sale at Amazon.com.

This chapter shows you how to use the Shop app to buy a variety of things right from your Kindle Fire with a few taps.

In this chapter

Browsing the stores

The Shop app is a central place to access several different stores on your Kindle Fire. Launch the Shop app by tapping Shop on the Home screen's library navigation (A). At the top of the screen is a Search Store box. Tapping it takes you to the stores search (covered in Chapter 3). Below that is a large picture promoting products that Amazon wants to draw to your attention. Swipe left and right with your finger to cycle through the four different promotions. Notice the four dots at the bottom of the promotion; they let you know the position of the promotion you're currently viewing. Tap anywhere on a promotion to go to the item it is representing.

At the bottom of the screen are all the stores you can browse. The digital stores are grouped together on the left:

- Books
- Music
- Videos
- Newsstand

- Apps
- Games
- Audiobooks

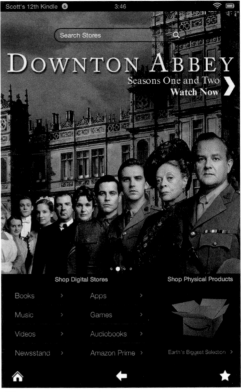

A The Shop app provides access to all the storefronts Amazon has to offer, as well as highlighting new or notable content.

Amazon Prime

Amazon Prime is a $79 yearly membership program. Membership includes the following:

- Free two-day shipping on Prime-eligible items denoted by the Prime logo **amazon** *Prime*.

- Discounted expedited shipping ($3.99 per item for one-day shipping for a weekday delivery and $8.99 for Saturday delivery).

- Access to an ever-expanding streaming video library called Prime Instant Videos (all of which you can watch on your Kindle Fire).

- The ability to borrow one e-book a month from the Kindle Owners' Lending Library. You can keep the book for as long as you like, but you can have only one book out at a time and borrow only once a month.

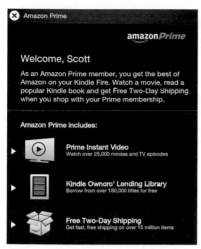

B Amazon Prime membership has its benefits. If you aren't a Prime member, you can sign up right from your Fire.

C The Amazon storefront looks very similar to Amazon.com.

Tapping any of these takes you to that specific digital store. These stores are covered in the chapters devoted to the library of the same name.

What happens when you tap the Amazon Prime store depends on whether you're signed up for a membership. If you are a Prime member, it reminds you of all the benefits to membership and highlights some content available to Prime members **B**. If you aren't a Prime member, you can sign up right from this screen.

TIP The Kindle Fire experience is greatly enhanced by an Amazon Prime membership. If you are a fairly frequent Amazon.com shopper, you'll find the free two-day shipping a delight.

Finally, in the lower far-right corner is the button for Amazon's physical products store (also known as Amazon.com).

To order physical goods from Amazon on your Kindle Fire:

1. Tap Shop on the Home screen's library navigation.

2. Tap the Shop Physical Products button.

3. This takes you to a rather familiar-looking storefront **C**. The front page contains items from your Wish Lists; swipe left and right to scroll through them. You'll also find recommended items, what other customers are looking at, and a section that shows particularly popular items.

continues on next page

4. Tap any item of interest to get more details .

5. On the Item Detail screen, you can read the product description, see the price, and look at reviews. Once you've decided you want to purchase the item, tap either Add to Cart or Buy Now with 1-Click, and select the shipping you want.

TIP If you have 1-Click enabled, that's all you need to do. The item has been ordered and will be shipped to your 1-Click address.

6. After you add an item to your cart, tap Continue Shopping or Go to Cart **E**. If you opt to continue shopping, you can always get to your cart by tapping the Cart icon at the top of the screen.

7. When looking at your cart, the subtotal is displayed at the top, with the items in your cart listed below **F**. To change the quantity of an item you're purchasing, tap the number and enter a new one with the onscreen keypad **G**. Tap Done when you're finished.

D An item's entry page gives you information about it, the chance to purchase it, and reviews to read.

E After you add an item to your cart, you can continue to shop, add even more to your cart, or just go to your cart and check out.

F The cart lists all of the items that you've placed in it, along with buttons to delete it or save it for later.

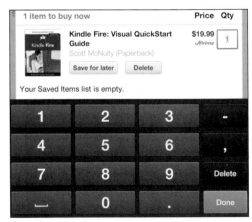

G Change the quantity of any item in your cart.

1 item saved for later	Price
Kindle Fire: Visual QuickStart Guide Scott McNulty (Paperback) [Move to Cart] [Delete]	$19.99 ✓Prime

Saved items appear in the lower section of the cart and can be added by tapping Move to Cart.

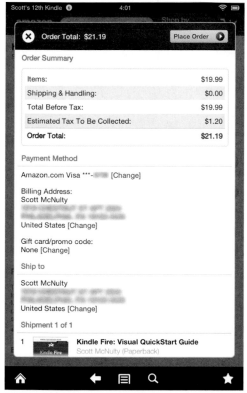

Scott's 12th Kindle 4:01

⊗ Order Total: $21.19   Place Order ▶

Order Summary

Items:	$19.99
Shipping & Handling:	$0.00
Total Before Tax:	$19.99
Estimated Tax To Be Collected:	$1.20
Order Total:	$21.19

Payment Method

Amazon.com Visa ***-   [Change]

Billing Address:
Scott McNulty

United States [Change]

Gift card/promo code:
None [Change]

Ship to

Scott McNulty

United States [Change]

Shipment 1 of 1

| 1 | Kindle Fire: Visual QuickStart Guide
Scott McNulty (Paperback) | |

Your order summary includes the order total, payment method, and shipping address (blurred in this picture for privacy reasons).

scott mcnu ⊗

scott mcnulty

scott mcnulty
in Books

Enter some text in the Search box to browse across the store for items.

If you no longer want to buy an item, tap Delete. To save an item for later consideration, tap Save for Later. The item is moved to your saved list and out of your cart (tap Move to Cart if you change your mind) .

8. Once you're happy with your cart's contents, tap Checkout. You'll need to supply your Amazon account and tap the Sign In button to continue.

9. An order summary with the total price, taxes, and shipping costs is displayed along with the payment method and the shipping address . Change either of these by tapping the Change link and selecting either another payment method or address.

TIP You can't pay for things using points accrued from rewards programs via the Shop app. You can, however, enter gift card and promo codes by tapping the Change link under that section.

10. Tap Place Order. An e-mail is sent to whatever e-mail address is associated with your Amazon account.

To find something to buy:

- At the top of every screen in the Shop app is a Search field. Tap it and type the name of whatever it is you're looking for . Suggested terms appear; tap one to search for it or tap the orange magnifying glass on the keyboard to search using your exact terms.

  The search results are shown and can be filtered using the Refine button as in the stores search (see Chapter 3). Tap an item to see details about it.

TIP Tapping the Amazon logo in the upper-left corner of the screen brings you back to the store's front page.

continues on next page

- If you would rather browse by department, just tap Shop by Department and select a department from the list **K**. Once you're in a department, you can tap its name to see a list of subdepartments **L**.

To share a link to an item:

1. Locate an item in the Amazon store. Tap it to get to its detail page.

2. Tap the Share button.

3. A list of available methods of sharing appears **M**. This list will vary depending on the apps you have installed, but e-mail is always listed because it is a default app. Tap the method you would like to use.

4. A link to the selected item is pasted to the sharing app of your choice, waiting for you to share it with friends and family **N**.

K You can browse by department. Tap any department to see a sortable list of the best-selling items.

L Each department, in this case Books, has a number of subdepartments that you can browse as well.

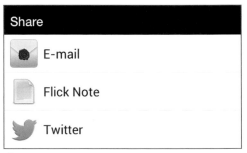

M The Share options depend on what apps you have installed, but you can always share via e-mail.

N A tweet created by the Share button includes a link to the item on Amazon.com.

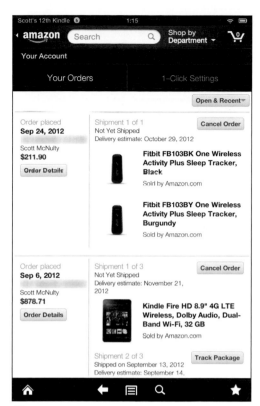

A All of your orders associated with your Amazon account are displayed here, arranged by most recently ordered at the top.

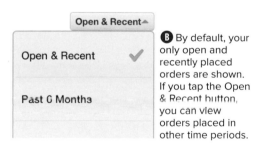

B By default, your only open and recently placed orders are shown. If you tap the Open & Recent button, you can view orders placed in other time periods.

Managing your account

You can't order anything from Amazon without an Amazon account (including the very Kindle Fire you're using). The Shop app gives you access to some of your account settings. The Shop app concentrates mostly on the order-related functions of your Amazon account, including enabling 1-Click Ordering.

To view and track your orders:

1. Open the Shop app (Home screen > Shop > Shop Physical Products).

2. Tap the menu icon on the navigation bar.

3. Tap Your Account.

4. You may be prompted for your Amazon account password. Enter it and tap Sign In.

5. Your Account page displays your recent and open (not yet shipped) orders in a scrollable list **A**. Swipe up and down to scroll through the list. If you want to filter your orders by a period of time, tap the Open & Recent button and select one of the options **B**.

continues on next page

A picture of the item ordered along with some of the order details are listed, including the price and the date the order was placed. If you need more detail about a specific order, tap Order Details **C**. Tap the x to close.

6. Tap Track Package to track your order **D**. Here, you can see shipping information such as the tracking code, delivery status, and shipper that was used. Tap the x to close.

⊗ Order Details

Order Date: Sep 17, 2012
Order #: ▓▓▓▓▓▓▓▓
Order Total: $6.99
Ship To: Scott McNulty
▓▓▓▓▓▓▓▓▓▓

Shipment #1: Delivery estimate: September 18, 2012

1 BlueRigger High Speed Micro HDMI to HDMI cable with Ethernet (6 Feet)
$6.99
BlueRigger LLC

Two-Day Shipping
Shipped on September 18, 2012

Ship my items as they become available

Payment Method

American Express *** ▓▓
Billing Address: ▓▓▓▓▓▓▓▓

Gift Card/Promo Code: None

Payment Information

Item(s) Subtotal:	$6.99
Shipping & Handling:	$0.00
Total Before Tax:	$6.99
Estimated Tax To Be Collected:	$0.00
Grand Total:	**$6.99**

C Order Details lists everything you want to know about one of your orders.

⊗ Shipment Tracking

Status: Unavailable
Ship Carrier: UPS
Tracking Number: ▓▓▓▓▓▓
Shipment Date: Oct 1, 2012
Destination:
Arrival Date: Oct 1, 2012

Track Your Package

Out for delivery
October 2, 2012 12:35:00 AM Philadelphia PA US

Arrival Scan
October 1, 2012 10:33:00 PM Philadelphia PA US

Departure Scan
October 1, 2012 9:43:00 PM Horsham PA US

Shipment received by carrier
October 1, 2012 12:58:00 PM Horsham PA US

D Tap the Track button, and you can locate your order.

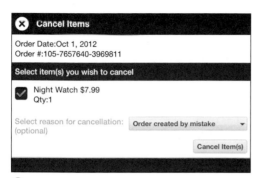

ⓔ The Cancel Order button is available only on open orders. Tap it to cancel the order.

ⓕ Tap the check mark next to the item, or items, that you want to cancel in the order. Then, tap Cancel Item(s).

To cancel an order:

1. Open the Shop app (Home screen > Shop > Shop Physical Products).

2. Tap the menu icon on the navigation bar.

3. Tap Your Account.

4. You may be prompted for your Amazon account password. Enter it and tap Sign In.

5. Locate the open order on the Your Orders list **ⓔ**.

6. Tap Cancel Order and enter a reason for the cancellation **ⓕ**. Tap the check box next to the item you don't want (this is useful for orders with multiple items) and tap Cancel Order. The order is removed from the Your Orders list and cancelled.

To modify your 1-Click settings:

1. Open the Shop app (Home screen > Shop > Shop Physical Products).

2. Tap the menu icon on the navigation bar.

3. Tap 1-Click Settings.

4. You may be prompted for your Amazon account password. Enter it and tap Sign In.

5. Your current 1-Click settings are displayed **G**.

   When 1-Click Ordering is turned on, you do not need to enter your Amazon password when placing an order. The order is also charged to a default credit card and shipped to a default address, so no interaction is required. (1-Click ordered items bypass the shopping cart.) If 1-Click is enabled, there will be a button labeled Turn OFF 1-Click. Tapping it will disable 1-Click on this device and change the button to read Turn ON 1-Click. Tap it again to enable 1-Click.

6. To change the address and credit card used by 1-Click, tap the Change link. Select an address from the list associated with your Amazon account and a payment method **H**. No need to confirm; the setting is changed immediately.

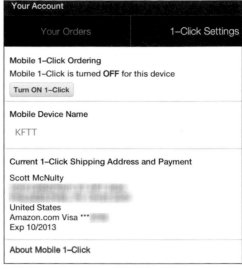

G You can change your 1-Click Settings right from your Kindle Fire.

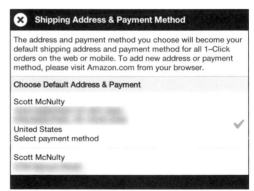

H Modify your 1-Click shipping address and payment method.

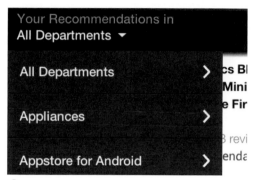

A Amazon uses many data points about your shopping habits to create a list of recommended things you might want to buy.

B Filter recommendations by department to see only recommended books or music, for example.

Using recommendations

Amazon is famous for its recommendation engine. That's the bit of technology used to predict what you might be interested in based on a combination of what you've purchased, the items in your Wish List, and the reviews and ratings you've left on Amazon.com. You can access the list of items Amazon recommends to you right from your Fire, and you can even help Amazon improve it.

To view your recommendations:

1. Open the Shop app (Home screen > Shop > Shop Physical Products).

2. Tap the menu icon on the navigation bar.

3. Tap Recommendations.

4. Swipe up and down to scroll through the list of recommendations **A**.

    These recommendations span all of Amazon's departments. If you want to see just the recommendations from a particular department, tap the Department drop-down, and then tap the department name **B**.

5. Tap an item to see details about it and to purchase it.

To improve your recommendations:

1. Open the Shop app (Home screen > Shop > Shop Physical Products).

2. Tap the menu icon on the navigation bar.

3. Tap Recommendations.

4. When you spot a recommendation that doesn't ring true or if you see an item that you own already, tap "Fix this recommendation."

5. Two buttons appear: "I own it" and "Not Interested" 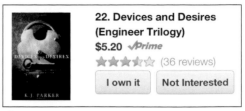. Tapping "I own it" lets Amazon know that you really are into items like this, and "Not Interested" tells Amazon not to recommend things like this to you.

6. The item disappears from your Recommendations list, and Amazon's servers know just a little bit more about you (in order to serve you better).

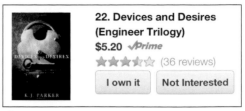

C Recommendations aren't always spot on, so you can fix them by tapping Fix This Recommendation and then tapping "I own it" or "Not Interested."

5

Games

Games are so important to the Kindle Fire experience that they have their own library. This is interesting because all Kindle Fire games are apps, and they show up in the Apps library in addition to the Games library. As you would expect, a ton of games are available for your Kindle Fire (many of them, free).

Games that support Amazon GameCircle, Amazon's social gaming network, allow you to compare your high scores with other players, sync your place in games across devices, and collect virtual tokens for game-related achievements.

This chapter covers downloading games, launching them, and getting social with Amazon GameCircle.

In this chapter

Getting games

Before you can play, or manage, a game on your Fire, you need to get some onto the device. Amazon has a wide variety of games available for download from your Kindle Fire.

To use the Game Store on the Kindle Fire:

1. Tap Games on the Home screen library navigation.

2. Tap Store in the upper-right corner of the screen .

3. The Games section of the Appstore appears . The Home screen of the Games section is broken up into five parts: the Search box, the section navigation, featured games, Top free and Paid games, and New Releases. Swipe up and down to scroll through the store, and swipe left and right to scroll through the various game groups. If you want to see only a particular type of game, tap that genre (Action, for example) in the section navigation.

Games has an icon that represents its name, average review (with number of reviews in parentheses), and price.

You can search the Appstore by tapping the Search box and typing in a query. As you type, suggestions appear . Tap one of them to search for that query, or tap the magnifying glass to search for the exact query you entered.

App results are displayed in a grid 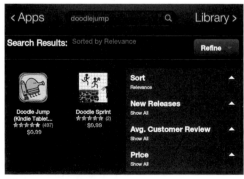. You can filter the results by tapping the Refine button and selecting one, or any combination, of the available filters.

A The Games library gathers together all your Fire games, both on the device and in the cloud.

B The Amazon Appstore has a variety of games available for download.

C When you search for a game, a list of suggestions, based on available games, is displayed.

D Once search results are shown, tap the Refine button to filter the results by a variety of criteria.

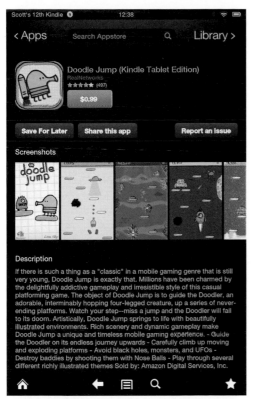

4. Tap an app's icon (or featured graphic) to get more information **E**. The game's icon is once again displayed along with the name, developer, rating, and price.

Swipe left and right to look at the screenshots from the game and get a feel for gameplay. The description, under the screenshots, is written by the makers of the game to convince you to take a chance and purchase the game.

Swipe to scroll down and see a list of games purchased by people who also bought this game **F**. Tap any of these games to see more information about them. Further down is a selection of customer reviews along with a summary of the various stars people have given the game. If you want to read all of the reviews, tap the "See all reviews" button.

continues on next page

E A game's entry in the Appstore includes the price, screenshots, and a description of the game.

F Further down the game's entry, related games are listed. Customer reviews appear below.

Even further down are the last four sections of the game entry: Permissions, Product Details, Developer Info, and a list of other apps by the same developer **G**. Permissions lists what the game has access to when installed on your Kindle Fire. This game, for example, will be able to access the network, write to your Fire's internal memory, and prevent it from going into a power-saving mode while the game is being played. Product Details lists the rating for the game, file size, ASIN (that's a unique number Amazon assigns to each app), release date, and version number. The final two sections give you some information about the developer of the game and the other games they've made.

5. After processing all of this information, tap the Price button next to the app's icon to buy it. When you tap the button, it turns green and reads Get App **H**.

6. Tap Get App to purchase the game and start downloading it **I**.

7. If you stay on the game's Appstore screen after it finishes downloading, an Open button appears **J**. Tap this button to launch your newly purchased game.

G At the bottom of every app entry is the list of permissions the game needs to run, product details (including the game's rating), and a list of other games made by the same company.

H Tap the price, and it turns into a green Get App button.

I After you purchase a game, it starts to download with the progress displayed.

J Once the game is finished downloading, tap Open to start playing.

K Email is the only option available for sharing an app from your Fire.

L Tapping Email in the Sharing menu opens a new e-mail and inserts the game's name plus a link with some text.

To share a link to a game:

1. Go to the Games section of the App-store on your Fire (Home screen > Games > Store).

2. Locate the game that you want to share a link to.

3. Tap the Share button on that game's entry.

4. Tap Email **K**.

5. A new e-mail message is created with a canned message and a link to the game **L**.

5. Fill out the rest of the e-mail, edit the message, and send it.

To download a game you've already purchased:

- All of your purchased games are listed in the Cloud section of your Games library (Home screen > Games > Cloud). Any game with a check on it has been downloaded to your device . Tap a game without a check to start downloading . A progress indicator appears on the icon of the game until it finishes downloading, at which time a check is displayed.

- On a previously purchased but not downloaded game's entry in the Kindle Fire App, a Store Download button appears . Tap the button to download the game to your device.

To launch a game:

1. Go to your Games library (Home screen > Games).

2. Locate the game that you want to play. Tap it, and if the game is on your device, it will open. If the game is on, your Cloud library has to download before you can launch it. Once the download is complete, tap the icon again and start playing the game.

TIP Each game for the Kindle Fire has a wildly different interface, so this book will not cover how to play particular games on your Fire.

M The game on the left, Temple Run, is in the Cloud library but not installed on the device. Bad Piggies has a check mark, meaning it is installed on the Fire and is ready to play.

N Downloading a game you own from the cloud is as simple as a tap. The download progress is displayed on the icon.

O When you view a game's Appstore entry and you already own it, a Download button is displayed.

P Games often hide the navigation bar. Tap this handle to reveal them.

Q The traditional in-app navigation bar. Tap the Home icon to return to the Home screen.

R In App Purchasing lets you spend money on game items without leaving the game. All items are charged to your Amazon account.

To access the navigation bar when in a game:

1. Most games will hide the standard navigation bar, so if you want to get back to the Home screen, you need to unhide it. Locate the small handle icon, either at the bottom or right side of the screen, while your game is running **P**.

2. Tap it to reveal the navigation bar complete with Home, Back, and Favorite buttons **Q**. These buttons work just as they do in other apps.

TIP Games that support GameCircle might also display a GameCircle icon in the navigation bar.

To purchase features in a game:

1. Each game sports a different look, but many offer additional items (levels, coins, characters) for purchase within the game. These items make use of a feature called In App Purchasing and are often offered via a store in the game. Look for a button labeled Store, or something like it, on the game's Home screen.

TIP Anything purchased via In App Purchasing charges you a fee in addition to the price of the game.

2. The contents of the in Appstore will differ from game to game, but each will list items and prices. Tap the item you want to purchase.

3. The Amazon In App Purchasing screen appears **R**. Tap the price to complete the purchase. Your Amazon account will be charged, and the new content is now available in your game. Tap the Cancel button if you decide not to complete the purchase, and you'll be taken back to the game, sans extra content.

Managing your games

Generally speaking, games for your Kindle Fire don't cost a lot of money, so you'll probably download your fair share. Soon enough, your Games library will become cluttered with a number of games, some of which you won't be interested in playing anymore. Luckily, you can sort your games, view them in a couple of ways, remove them from your Fire, and totally delete them by going to Amazon.com.

To sort your games:

1. Open your Games library (Home screen > Games).

2. Tap the Menu button on either the Cloud or Device tab. The sort settings apply to both libraries no matter which one is active when you apply it 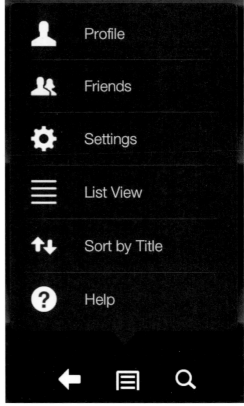.

3. There are two sorting options: Sort by Title and Sort by Date. Sort by Title will arrange your games in alphabetical order. Sort by Date arranges them by most recently interacted with. This means recently downloaded and launched games will appear at the top of the library.

4. Tap the Sort menu item to toggle between Sort by Date and Sort by Title.

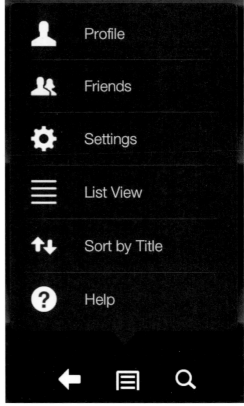

Ⓐ The Games library menu allows you to change views.

B List View displays additional information about GameCircle games.

C Long tap a game to see this menu. Tap Remove from Device to delete it.

To change between List and Grid Views:

1. Open your Games library (Home screen > Games).

2. Tap the Menu button on either the Cloud or Device tab **A**.

3. By default. your Games library is displayed in Grid view, with each game's icon sitting on virtual shelves. Tap List View in the menu to switch views **B**. List view respects whatever sorting you've applied, but also shows a little more information. The blue icons are all related to Amazon GameCircle (see the next section) and are displayed only on games that offer GameCircle support.

4. Tap the Menu icon and then Grid View to change back.

To remove a game:

1. Open your Games library (Home screen > Games).

2. Tap the Device tab or look for a game icon that displays the check mark signifying it has been downloaded to your device.

3. Long tap the downloaded game you want to remove from your Kindle Fire **C**.

4. Tap Remove from Device. The game is deleted from your Fire's storage, and the check mark is removed from its icon.

To delete a game from your account:

1. Open Amazon.com in the browser of your choice (on a computer or in Silk on your Fire).

2. Click the Your Account button at the top right of the site **D**.

3. Click the Your Android Apps & Devices link.

4. All of your app purchases, including games, are listed on this page **E**. By default, the list of apps is sorted by name, but if you click the "Sort by" menu, you can change to Sort to Purchase Date and Developer in addition to Title.

5. Next to each app is an Actions button. Click it to reveal the actions you can take **F**.

6. Click Delete, and a warning appears letting you know that this will permanently delete the app **G**. If you've paid for this app, you'll need to buy it again to use it. You'll also lose any In App Purchasing that you've done. If you're sure, click the Delete button.

7. The app is deleted from your account and will no longer show up in your Fire's Games library.

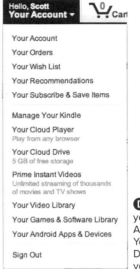

D You can manage your apps via Amazon.com in the Your Android Apps & Devices section of your account.

E The list of all the apps you've downloaded from Amazon's Appstore

F The Actions menu includes "Delete this app."

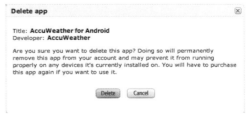

G Deleting an app via this method completely removes it, and in-app purchases, from your account.

A When creating your GameCircle profile, select a user name and an avatar.

B Your GameCircle account displays your nickname. Tap Edit to change it whenever you want.

Using Amazon GameCircle

Amazon GameCircle is a set of services that Amazon provides to game developers. If a developer chooses to support them in their games, they gain access to three features: in-game achievements, leaderboards, and WhisperSync.

When WhisperSync is enabled, your game progress is synced wirelessly to all of your GameCircle-supported devices. This is similar to how your reading position is synced via WhisperSync to all your Kindles when you're reading a book.

Not all games support these features, but more and more are adding GameCircle support.

TIP Visit http://amazon.com/gamecircle-games to see a full list of GameCircle games.

To set up your profile:

1. Go to your Games library (Home screen > Games).

2. Tap the Menu button and then Profile.

3. Amazon creates a nickname for you automatically and assigns you a Profile icon **A**. This nickname will be displayed on the leaderboards.

4. Type a new name or keep the one that Amazon randomly picked. Swipe left or right to browse the available profile images. The image in the middle of the group is the one that will be associated with your account. Tap Update, and your profile is complete **B**.

TIP You can change your nickname and avatar at any point by tapping Profile and then tapping Edit.

To find your friends on GameCircle:

1. Go to your Games library (Home screen > Games).

2. Tap the Menu icon and then Friends.

3. Tap the Add Friends button **C**.

4. Enter your friend's GameCircle nickname and tap the orange magnifying glass on the keyboard **D**.

5. Your friend's GameCircle profile is displayed, including what games they are playing and the number of friends they have **E**.

6. Tap Friend to send a friend request. You will be notified if your request is approved, and the person will show up in your Friends list.

C If you've added friends on GameCircle, they will show up here. Tap Add Friends to search for a friend.

D GameCircle friend search. Type in a nickname to find someone.

E Looking at someone else's profile shows you what games you have in common.

F GameCircle games display these four icons when your Games library is in List View.

G An example of an in-app alert about earning two achievements

To determine whether a game supports GameCircle:

1. Go to your Games library (Home screen > Games).

2. Make sure your Games library is in List View.

3. Any game with four blue icons next to it supports GameCircle **F**. The blue icons represent, from left to right, your friends who play this particular game; the number of achievements you have out of the number available; your position in the leaderboard; and a summary of all GameCircle-related things for that game.

To earn achievements:

1. Every GameCircle game offers different achievements that are awarded to you when you meet some sort of milestone: score 10,000 points, jump on six enemies in a row, and so on. The achievements have a direct relation to gameplay.

2. As you play and meet the criteria for an achievement, it is automatically awarded to you, and a small alert appears **G**.

TIP If you want to see which achievements are available in a game, make sure your Games library is in List View; then tap the Achievements icon next to the game that interests you.

To view leaderboards and achievements:

- In List View of your Games library, tap the Achievements icon next to the game that interests you **H**. When in Grid View, a Summary item appears in the menu of GameCircle games when you long tap them **I**.

  All of the achievements available in the game are listed, and the achievements that you've earned are highlighted **J**. Swipe up and down to scroll through the whole list.

H The Achievements icon

I Long tap a game's icon. If the game supports GameCircle, you'll see Summary listed.

J The Achievements list shows you both achievements you've earned and those you still need to earn.

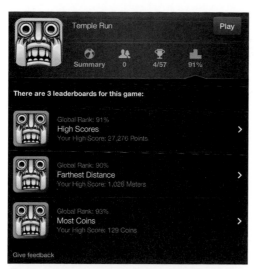

K Each game can have multiple leaderboards based on different aspects of gameplay.

L All of the leaderboards display the same information: time-based charts of the best players of the game, with your best scores shown, and how you rank compared to the rest of the players.

Tap the Leaderboard icon to check out how you're doing as compared to players worldwide **K**. A game can have multiple leaderboards that track different aspects of the game, but each board has the same features: the stats for today, this week, and all time **L**. Tap one to see a list of players and how you stack up. Tap the Top 100 button to see the top 100 players' stats with yours displayed so that you can compare.

continues on next page

Summary View gives you a thumbnail view of your standings on the leaderboard, the top players, and your next earnable achievement ⓜ. Tap the Summary icon to see it.

- Each game has a slightly different way of presenting your achievements within the game. Many games have a Stats section or an icon of a trophy to denote achievements. When you tap it, a standardized GameCircle screen appears. It gives you access to all the same information available in the GameCircle screen accessed from the Games library ⓝ. Tap the x button to return to the game.

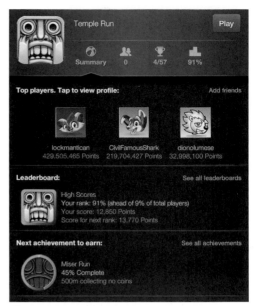

ⓜ The GameCircle Summary lists your high scores, the top players, and the next achievement you can earn.

ⓝ The in-app GameCirle summary looks very much the same; however, if you tap the x, you return to your game.

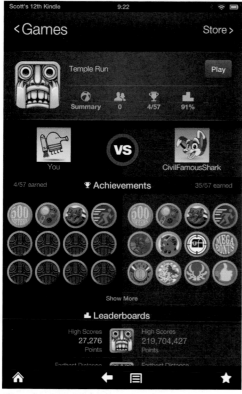

O When viewing someone's profile on GameCircle, the games you have in common are listed.

P Comparing game achievements and scores with another GameCircle profile

To compare your game stats with someone else on GameCircle:

1. Go to your Games library (Home screen > Games).

2. If your Games library is in Grid View, long tap the game in which you want to compare yourself to a friend; then tap Summary.

   If your Games library is in List View, tap the Friends icon next to the game that interests you.

3. Select the friend you want to compare yourself to from the list.

   You can also compare yourself to people on a game's leaderboard by tapping their names to get to their profiles.

4. On your friend's profile, tap the Compare button next to the game that you both play. If you and your friend don't play any of the same games, you can't compare yourself to them **O**.

5. Your achievements and leaderboard positions are shown on the left while your friend's are on the right **P**.

To modify GameCircle settings:

1. Go to your Games library (Home screen > Games).

2. Tap the Menu icon in the navigation bar and then tap Settings.

3. The Amazon GameCircle settings allow you to hide your nickname (effectively turning off GameCircle), turn off the Facebook connection, and disable WhisperSync for Games .

   Tap Hide next to Share your Game-Circle Nickname, and you'll become invisible to everyone on GameCircle, including friends. You won't be able to compare your stats to those of other players either, but your own stats will still be tracked. You can view them and collect achievements.

   Tap Off on Facebook to stop sharing your stats on GameCircle with your Facebook profile (using your real name). Tap On to reenable Facebook integration.

   Finally, you may no longer want to sync your game state to your other Amazon GameCircle-compatible devices. (At the moment, this is limited to other Kindle Fires and Android phones that support the Amazon Appstore.) Just tap Off. You can turn syncing back on at any time by tapping On.

Ⓠ The GameCircle settings allow you to hide your nickname (basically turning off GameCircle) and toggle Facebook integration as well as WhisperSync.

6

Apps

Apps, short for applications, are little pro-grams that add functionality to your Kindle Fire. Thousands of apps are available in the Amazon Appstore, designed especially to take advantage of the Kindle Fire's larger screen.

Apps range from games (covered in Chapter 5) to magazines to apps that allow you to log into a computer remotely, some-where else in the world.

Amazon decides which apps are allowed into the Amazon Appstore. You can down-load with confidence that you aren't going to install an app from Amazon that will mess up your Fire.

You do need an active wireless connection to connect to the Appstore on your Fire and a valid Amazon account.

In this chapter

Getting apps

The easiest way to get apps for your Kindle Fire is to purchase them from the Amazon Appstore. You can also load apps from other sources onto your Kindle Fire. These apps are known as *third-party apps*.

To browse the Kindle Fire Appstore:

1. Go to your Apps library (Home screen > Apps).

2. Tap the Store button at the top of the library .

3. This takes you to the front page of the Amazon Appstore, which looks a lot like the Games store described in Chapter 5 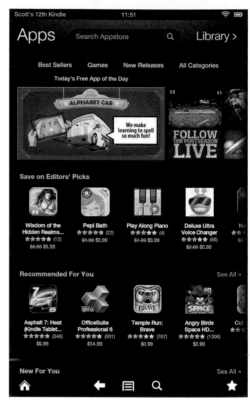. This is because the Games store is just a subsection of the Amazon Appstore.

   The front page is broken up into a few sections: Search, categories, promoted apps. There are also sections of high-lighted apps that usually are included in Recommended For You and New For You. Finally, there is a section that changes (in this figure, highly rated games are shown).

TIP Amazon offers up one paid app a day for free. It is featured on the front page of the Appstore and is labeled Today's Free App of the Day.

A The Apps library with the Cloud library selected and sorted by title

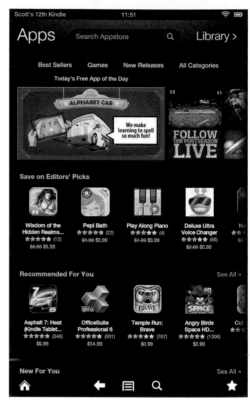

B The Amazon Appstore on the Kindle Fire. Notice the big promotional image for Today's Free App of the Day.

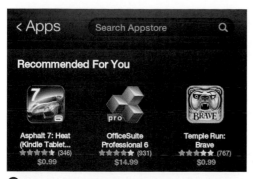

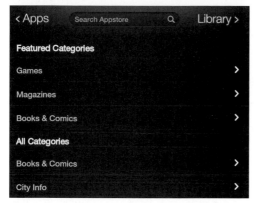

C Each section of the Appstore lists apps in a grid

D The available categories in the Appstore

Swipe your finger back and forth to scrub through the apps in each section. Some of the sections show a few of the apps that are available. If you want to see all the apps in a section, tap See All **C**.

Tap any of the categories at the top of the screen to see all the apps listed. The Best Sellers category is a great way to find lots of high-quality apps that other people are using. It is broken up into a few subcategories including Top Paid, Top Free, and Top Rated (these are apps that might be free or paid but have received lots of good reviews).

Tap the All Categories button, or tap Menu > All Categories, to see every category on the Appstore **D**. Tap any of the categories on the list to see the apps that make up the category.

4. Tap an app you're interested in down-loading to see details about it.

To search the Kindle Fire Appstore:

1. If browsing the Appstore isn't getting you the app you want, you can always search as well. Tap the Search box and start typing. Suggestions will appear .

2. Tap one of the suggestions to search for it. As an alternative, tap the magnifying glass icon next to the Search box, or tap the keyboard to search the phrase exactly as entered.

3. Tap the Refine button to change the sorting of the search results and to apply a combination of the available filters **F**.

4. Tap an app to get more information about it.

TIP When you're browsing a category in the Appstore, the Search box will limit its searches to just that category.

E Searching the Appstore works much like searching elsewhere on your Fire.

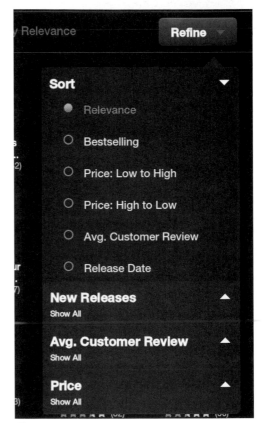

F Refine your search results by selecting a sort and any number of filters.

continues on next page

G An app's entry in the Appstore displays lots of information. The first section lists price, screenshots, and a description.

To purchase/download an app from the Amazon Appstore on your Kindle Fire:

1. Once you've found an app you're interested in, you'll notice that its product page on the Appstore has lots of information about it **G**. At the top of the page are the app's icon and name, plus its star ranking and the number of reviews it has received. Under those is a button that displays the app's price (free or a dollar amount).

   Next, three buttons allow you to save this app for later, share it, or report an issue with the app to Amazon. Below those are screenshots, uploaded by the developer, that give you a sense of what the app's interface looks like. Tap one to view it full screen (tap again to return to the app's entry).

Sideloading applications

Sideloaded apps are installed from somewhere other than the Amazon Appstore. Amazon would prefer that you purchase any apps for your Fire directly from Amazon. This does have advantages:

- All apps purchased from Amazon are stored in your Cloud Apps library. They are just a tap away from being installed on any Fire device associated with your Amazon account.

- Amazon tests and vets all the apps listed in their store, so you know you aren't going to get any nasty surprises from those apps.

- The Appstore on the Fire is easy to search and browse and contains thousands of apps.

However, there are valid reasons why you might want to install an app from what Amazon calls "unknown sources," mostly to scare you away from doing it. You should think carefully before following the instructions in the next section. No one inspects apps from "unknown sources," and you could possibly install an app that does something you aren't aware of. Install apps only from trusted sources.

The app developer enters the description, which is the big block of text under the screenshots. Generally, it tells you a bit about the app's features, how neat it is, and if it has won any distinctions (such as an award from a magazine or being featured by Amazon in the Appstore).

Scroll down to see a few apps that people who bought this app also purchased . Tap any of those app icons to go to its entry. Under that are the reviews of this app, summarized by a handy chart, which breaks down the star ratings. Tap "See all reviews" to display them, and tap "Create your own review" to leave your own.

The final third of the app's entry lists the permissions the app needs to work on your Fire; product details including rating, app version, and size of the download; and a list of other apps made by the same developers (if any) 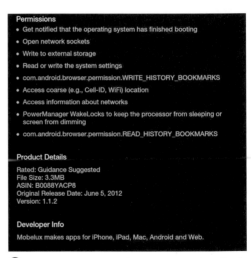.

2. Tap the orange button next to the app icon to purchase it .

3. The button turns into a green Get App button after it is tapped .

4. Tap the green button to purchase the app. If you stay on the app entry, the download progress will be displayed.

TIP Your Amazon account is charged for the app, and a receipt is e-mailed to you.

5. Once the app is finished downloading and installing, a notification appears. The button on the app entry also turns into an Open button.

H Further down the entry, you'll find similar apps and reviews.

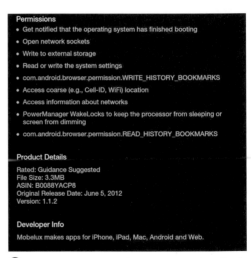

I Permissions, Product Details (such as File Size), and Developer Info round out an app's entry.

J The price button for a $2.99 app

K After tapping the orange price button, it turns into the green Get App button.

Allow Installation of Applications
From unknown sources   **On**   Off

L If you want to install apps from sources other than the Amazon Appstore, turn on this setting.

Warning

When you use applications from unknown sources, your Kindle and personal data are less secure and there is a risk of unexpected behavior. You agree that you are solely responsible for any damage to your Kindle or loss of data that may result from using these applications.

| Cancel | OK |

M Amazon warns you that apps from unknown sources have the potential to damage your Fire. Exercise caution.

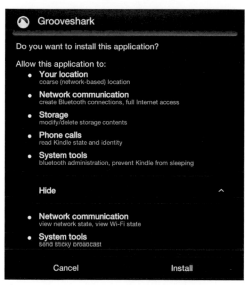

N The first thing you see when installing an app from an unknown source is a list of the permissions it requires.

O Installing an app from an unknown source

To install an app from somewhere other than the Amazon Appstore:

1. Swipe down from the top of the device and tap More on Quick Settings.

2. Tap Device.

3. Tap On next to Allow Installation of Applications from unknown sources **L**.

4. Read the warning and tap OK **M**.

5. Now, you can install any Android app as long as you have the APK file that makes up the app. You can find these on the Internet with some searching or on app developer sites directly. Download the file to your Fire (either via e-mail or using Silk) and tap it **N**.

6. Read the permissions that the app requires. If you're OK with the requirements, tap Install **O**.

7. Tap Open to access the app **P**. It is also listed in your Device Apps library. The app will not be in your Cloud library because you didn't purchase it from Amazon.

P When the app finishes installing, tap Open to launch it.

Using apps

Similar to a game, each app has a unique user interface. This book won't explain how to use particular apps. However, this section covers launching apps, adding them to your Favorites, changing preferences, managing notifications, and reviewing an app after you've used it for some time.

To launch an app:

- Your Apps library has two sections: Cloud and Device. To launch apps from the Device section, go to your Apps library (Home screen > Apps) and tap the Device tab . Tap any of the apps listed here, and they will launch immediately.

- Launching apps from the Cloud library (Home screen > Apps > Cloud) is very similar with one difference. The Cloud library lists all your Fire apps, whether or not they've been downloaded to your device. Before you can launch an app, it must be downloaded to the device.

  Apps with a check mark on their icon in your Cloud library have been downloaded and can be launched with a tap **B**. Apps without the check mark must be downloaded first, by tapping them. The download progress is displayed on the app **C**. Once the download is complete, the icon gets a check mark. Then, you can tap the app to launch it.

A The Device Apps library lists only apps installed on the device.

B When in the Cloud library, which lists all apps you've purchased, apps installed on the device have a check mark on the icon.

C Download progress is displayed on the app's icon.

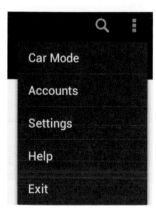

D Long tap an app's icon to access this menu.

E The Menu icon is available in some apps, and this is where you'll find the settings/preferences.

F Some apps have this icon with three squares at the top right of the screen, which is where the menu is located.

To add an app to your Favorites:

1. Long tap the app either in your Apps library (Home screen > Apps) or on the Carousel of the Home screen.

2. Tap Add to Favorites **D**. Now, the app is always one tap away from being launched.

TIP You can add apps that you haven't downloaded from your Cloud library to your Favorites using the same method. The first time you tap the app in Favorites, it'll download. Tap again to launch it.

To access an app's preferences:

- Each app presents its preferences (some call them *settings*) in different ways. The traditional way of accessing preferences within a Kindle Fire app is via the Menu button on the navigation bar (which might be hidden; if so, tap the small handle at the bottom of the screen to reveal the navigation bar) **E**.

- Some apps have a button with three squares in the top-right corner of the screen. Tap it to reveal a menu that will contain an option for settings/ preferences if the app has them **F**.

- Some apps don't have any settings/ preferences that you can change.

To turn off an app's notifications:

1. When you install an app, you are allowing it to send notifications to you via the built-in Notifications system (see Chapter 1). Swipe down to access Quick Settings and then tap More.

2. Tap Applications .

3. Tap Notification Settings to see a list of all the apps installed on your Kindle Fire and their current notification settings.

4. Notifications are a binary situation: They are either on or off for an app. When notifications are on, that app can send messages to the notifications area when any number of things happen. When they are off (tap Off next to the app), no notifications from that app will be sent. You can have some apps with notifications off and others with notifications enabled.

G The Applications settings for the Fire

H The Notification Settings area allows you to disable or enable notifications on a per-app basis.

A The current sort applied to the Apps library is displayed in orange.

Managing your apps

Apps have the power to transform your Kindle Fire into a sort of touchscreen Swiss Army knife: one tool with many purposes. The downside is that your Apps library will soon be bursting at the virtual seams with apps of all kinds. Your Kindle Fire has limited on-board storage. The Cloud library has unlimited space, but it only stores apps purchased from the Amazon Appstore. So, you're going to need some strategies for managing your apps. This section covers sorting your library, removing and deleting apps you no longer use, and force-quitting misbehaving apps. It also explains how to get more information about which apps are currently running and what they are doing.

To sort your Apps library:

1. Go to your Apps library (Home screen > Apps).

2. The current sort is shown in orange at the top of the Apps library (Cloud or Device) **A**.

3. There are two options: By Recent and By Title. Tap either to toggle back and forth. By Title arranges your apps alphabetically by title, and By Recent places the one interacted with most recently at the top. Recently launched and installed apps are listed before those apps you haven't used much.

TIP The sort option you choose applies to both of your libraries: Device and Cloud.

To remove an app from your device:

1. Find the app you want to remove from your Fire by going to your Apps library, searching for it, or finding it in the Carousel.

2. Long tap it.

3. Tap Remove from Device.

   The app no longer takes up storage space on your Fire, but it is still available from your Cloud library. The app must be downloaded again if you want to use it. Also, any in-app purchases you might have made are still available.

To delete an app:

1. Removing an app takes it off your Kindle Fire, but it still sticks around in your Cloud library. If you truly want to delete an app completely, you must log into Amazon.com and manage your apps from there.

2. Click Your Account on Amazon.com. Then click Your Android Devices and Apps **B**.

3. Log in with your Amazon account.

4. Find the app you want to delete from the list.

5. Click the Actions button next to the app you want to delete and then click "Delete this app" **C**.

6. A warning appears letting you know that this really deletes the app and all in-app purchases. If you want to use this app again, you'll need to download it and pay for it.

7. Click Delete to remove the app from your account. It will no longer show up in the Cloud library.

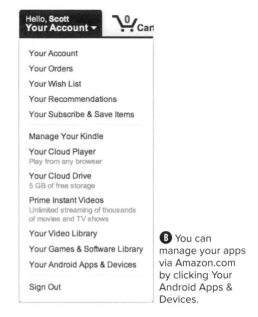

B You can manage your apps via Amazon.com by clicking Your Android Apps & Devices.

C Click "Delete this app" from the Actions menu to delete an app permanently from your Amazon account.

D The list of Installed Applications allows you to find out more about which apps are on your Fire.

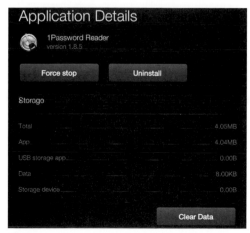

E You can filter the list to see only third-party applications or running applications.

F Here, you can see more information about this particular app, including the total storage that it takes up.

To find out which apps are running:

1. If you're curious about which apps are running on your Kindle Fire, swipe down to bring up Quick Settings and tap More.

2. Tap Applications.

3. Tap Installed Applications, which lists information about all the applications on your Fire. This includes apps that are part of the operating system **D**.

4. Tap the Filter By menu and tap Running Applications to see only apps that are running currently on your Fire **E**.

5. Tap an app to see more information about it, including exactly how much storage it takes up **F**.

To force-quit an app:

1. If an app misbehaves, you can force-quit it by going to the Running Applications list (as described earlier).

2. Tap the app that isn't responding in the list.

3. Tap the "Force stop" button, and a warning appears **G**.

4. Tap OK, and the app stops running.

5. Tap the app in the Apps library to launch it again.

G When you force-stop an app, it quits no matter what it is doing.

To see an app's permissions:

1. When you download an app from the Appstore, the entry lists the various permissions that the app needs in order to work. These include access to the wireless network, reading your contacts, and the like. After downloading an app, you can check its permissions by going into Applications Settings (Quick Settings > More > Applications > Installed Applications).

2. Tap the "Filter by" menu and tap Third-Party Applications to see only apps you've downloaded from the Appstore or unknown sources.

3. Tap the application you're interested in and scroll down until you see the Permissions section.

4. Tap "Show all" to see all the details about which permissions the app needs 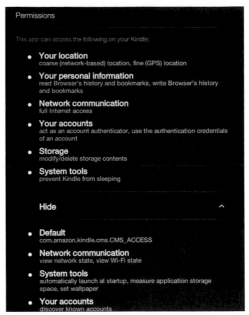.

H A detailed list of the permissions an app has on your Fire, and its data

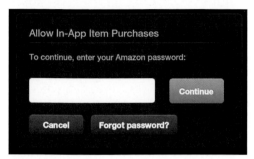

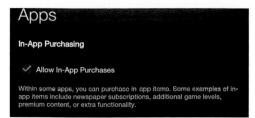

Apps

In-App Purchasing

✓ Allow In-App Purchases

Within some apps, you can purchase in-app items. Some examples of in-app items include newspaper subscriptions, additional game levels, premium content, or extra functionality.

ⓘ You can disable In-App Purchasing to prevent accidental purchases.

Allow In-App Item Purchases

To continue, enter your Amazon password:

Continue

Cancel   Forgot password?

ⓙ Turning off In-App Purchasing (or turning it back on) requires your Amazon password.

To disable In-App Purchasing:

1. Some apps, including games and magazines, offer things for sale within the app. To disable this setting, go to Applications Settings (Quick Settings > More > Applications).

2. Tap Appstore **ⓘ**.

3. Tap In-App Purchasing.

4. Uncheck Allow In-App Purchases **ⓘ**.

5. You must enter your Amazon password to disable (or enable) in-app purchases **ⓙ**. Enter your password and tap Continue.

6. In-app purchases are now disallowed.

TIP To re-enable in-app purchases, check the box, enter your Amazon password, and tap Continue.

To force your Kindle Fire to sync application content:

1. Your Fire automatically syncs with Amazon's cloud servers, updating your Cloud Apps library with purchases, and syncing any changes you've made on your device. If you need to force the sync process to start, open Applications Settings (Quick Settings > More > Applications).

2. Tap Sync Amazon Content. The two arrows will rotate as the syncing happens.

Updating apps

Developers are hard at work improving their apps day and night. They add new features, fix bugs, and refine the interface, all without charging you an additional fee (for the most part). Keeping your Fire's apps up to date isn't a tough job because out of the box it is handled automatically. If you want more control over your app updates, you can switch to manual updates.

To be alerted when an app has been updated automatically:

1. Open Applications Settings (Quick Settings > Applications).
2. Tap the Appstore Ⓐ.
3. Tap Automatic Updates Ⓑ. By default, automatic updates are enabled. Tap the check box next to Notify Me When Updates are Installed to be alerted when an app has been updated successfully.

TIP Uncheck this setting if you want your apps to update silently.

To turn off automatic updates:

1. Open Applications Settings (Quick Settings > Applications).
2. Tap the Appstore and then Automatic Updates.
3. Uncheck Enable Automatic Updates. This unchecks the notification setting automatically as well because no updates will be installed without your manual intervention.

To update an app manually:

1. A notification will display to alert you about available updates.
2. Tap the Update button to apply the updates.
3. The update is downloaded and applied.

TIP Sideloaded cannot be updated via the Fire's built-in update mechanism. You'll need to re-install the app every time an update is available.

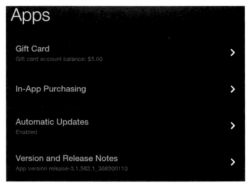

Ⓐ Appstore preferences

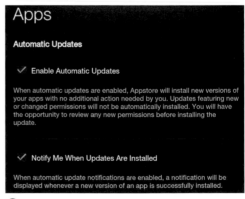

Ⓑ The options for Automatic Updates; by default, it is turned on.

7

Books

Before the Kindle platform included a number of tablets such as the Kindle Fire HD, it was all about reading. The Kindle Fire is true to its heritage: Reading on this device is a pleasure. It gives you access to hundreds of thousands of books from Amazon, not to mention ebooks from a large number of libraries and other retailers.

This chapter covers filling your Fire with ebooks, reading them, annotating them, and searching through them.

In this chapter

Getting books

Buying books on your Kindle Fire is pretty simple with its built-in Kindle Store. You can also purchase Kindle books on Amazon.com and have them sent directly to your Kindle Fire. However, Amazon isn't the only game in town when it comes to books for your Fire. Many libraries offer ebooks for loan via a company called OverDrive, and some publishers sell ebooks from their own websites that you can read on your Fire.

To use the Kindle Store on your Fire:

1. Make sure your Kindle Fire is connected to a wireless network.

2. Tap Books on the Home screen library navigation.

3. Tap Store.

4. The front page of the Kindle Store is organized into a number of sections: Recommended For You lists books you might like, based on your purchases; the Kindle Select 25 are 25 Kindle books selected by the editors of the Kindle Store; Best Sellers lists the best-selling books, and so on **A**. Tap See All to list every book in a particular section.

   Featured Lists, on the right side of the screen, displays books created by the Kindle Kindle Store editors. Above that is a Popular Categories button. Tap it to see some top-selling books from some hand-selected categories **B**. Tap See All to view all the books in that category.

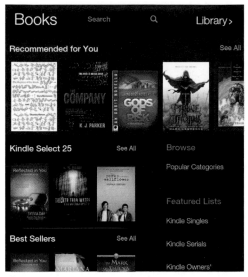

A The front page of the Kindle Store

B Books featured from a list of popular categories on the store

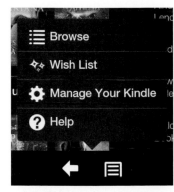

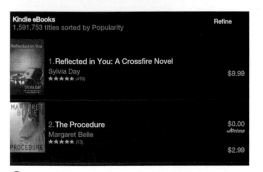

C Tap Browse in the menu to see all the book categories.

D All Kindle eBooks in one list, sorted by popularity

If you like to peruse books, tap the Menu button in the navigation to bring up the Browse button **C**. Tap this to see a full list of all the Kindle books available **D**. Tap the Refine button to select a particular category, sort option, and rating.

Finally, you can search the Kindle Store just like the other stores. Start typing a query in the Search box, and suggestions appear. Tap either one of the suggestions to search for that. Tap the magnifying glass to search for your exact phrase.

continues on next page

Buying books somewhere other than Amazon

Amazon is the easiest place to purchase books for your Kindle Fire. However, Amazon isn't the only game in town. You can purchase PDFs from a variety of sources, and you will have no trouble reading them on your Fire. In addition, many publishers offer their ebooks for sale directly from their own sites. You just need to look for the Kindle-compatible files (they will be marked as such). Also be sure that the books don't have any digital rights management (DRM) applied to them.

The Kindle Fire only supports books with DRM from Amazon; others will not work with your Kindle Fire. Also, many places sell ebooks in ePub format. The Kindle Fire does *not* support ePub. In order to read ebooks in ePub format on your Kindle, they must being converted into a Kindle-friendly format.

See the "Sideloading" section in this chapter to find out several ways of transferring non-Amazon ebooks to your Kindle.

5. Once you've found a book you're interested in, tap its cover to see more detail about it **E**. The book title, author, average rating, price, and cover are all displayed.

If you want to try a chapter of the book before you pay for it, tap Try a Sample. This sends a sample of the book to your Kindle Fire. You can read it and then buy the book right from the sample.

The rest of the book's entry includes a description, a list of related books you might want to buy as well, and the reviews (tap "See all reviews" to read them).

Tap "More about the author" at the bottom of the entry to read a biography, as well as some details about the book **F**. A Kindle book might list the Page # Source among the details. That means the Kindle book displays page numbers from the edition cited in the source. It also shows the traditional Kindle locations (see the "Reading books" section for more about this).

E A book's product page includes the cover, title, author, ratings, and price.

F More information about both the author and the book is located at the bottom of a book's page.

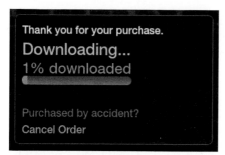

G After you purchase a book from the Kindle Store, the download progress is displayed.

H Once the download finishes, tap the "Read now" button to open the book.

I The Kindle Store on Amazon.com.

Product Details
File Size: 1857 KB
Print Length: 401 pages
Page Numbers Source ISBN: 0340963115
Publisher: VIKING ADULT (October 2, 2012)
Sold by: Penguin Publishing
Language: English
ASIN: B007V65QE6
Text-to-Speech: Enabled ☑
X-Ray: Enabled ☑
Amazon Best Sellers Rank: #2,339 Paid in Kindle Store (See Top 100 Paid in Kindle Store)

J Book details from Amazon.com

Buy now with 1-Click®
Deliver to:
✓ Scott's 10th Kindle
  Scott's 13th Kindle
  Scott's 3rd Kindle

K When purchasing a Kindle book from Amazon.com, you must indicate which Kindle should receive it.

6. Once you find a book you want to buy, tap the orange button that says "Buy for" with the price displayed on it.

7. The book downloads **G**.

8. The book is added to your Book library. Its entry in the store turns into a green "Read now" button **H**. Tap it to read the book.

TIP Newly purchased books also appear on the Carousel of the Home screen.

To use the Kindle Store on Amazon.com:

1. Go to Amazon.com, click Kindle, and then click Kindle Books in the Shop by Department menu.

2. The front page of the Kindle Store allows you to search, click any of the featured books, or browse by category **I**.

3. Click the book you're interested in to display more details about it. Scroll down to see whether the book offers real page numbers and if it supports Text-to-Speech, X-Ray (see the "Searching books and using X-Ray" section), and Lending **J**.

4. When you're sure you want to purchase the Kindle book, you have to tell Amazon which Kindle should receive the book. Select the Kindle from the dropdown list in the green price box **K**.

5. Once you have selected the book, click the Buy button. The book is purchased, added to your Kindle books Cloud library, and sent to the Kindle that you chose.

To borrow a book from the Kindle Owners' Lending Library:

1. The Amazon Prime Lending Library consists of thousands of books that only Amazon Prime members can borrow. (See Chapter 4 for more information about Amazon Prime.) You can borrow one book a month, but you can keep it for as long as you like. To find Amazon Prime Lending Library books, go to the Kindle Books Store (Home screen > Books > Store) and tap Kindle Owners' Lending Library.

2. Tap Refine and then Category to filter choices based on the book types .

3. Once you find a book you want to read, tap it and then tap Borrow for Free .

4. The book downloads and a message lets you know when you'll be able to borrow another book from the Kindle Owners' Lending Library.

TIP When a book from the Kindle Owners' Lending Library is returned, search results will display a little Prime logo to let you know it can be borrowed **N**.

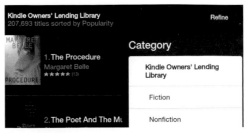

L Tap the Refine button to filter and sort any list of books in the Kindle Store.

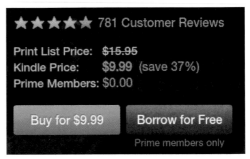

M Books in the Kindle Owners' Lending Library have a Borrow for Free button.

N The Prime logo in search results and listings indicates that this book is part of the Kindle Owners' Lending Library.

O A book's detail on a library website that supports OverDrive

P The final stage of borrowing a Kindle book from a library is handled on Amazon.com.

To borrow a book from your local library:

1. Borrowing ebooks from your library is simple, though it does require a couple of things. First, you need a library card and account to log into your library's website. Second, your library must be one of over 11,000 that offers services from a company called OverDrive. If you aren't sure whether your local library is an Overdrive library, check this website: http://search.overdrive.com.

2. Go to your library's website and look for their ebook catalog.

3. Click it and search for an ebook.

4. Add the Kindle format to your cart **O**. Continue browsing.

5. When you're finished, click "Proceed to checkout" in your cart. Then, enter your library card number and personal identification number. Your library will set these up for you if you don't have them.

6. Click Confirm Check Out and then Get for Kindle.

7. You're transferred to an Amazon page where you select the Kindle that should receive this ebook. Then, click "Get library book" **P**.

8. The book is added to your library and will be taken out at the end of the loan period. You'll also receive an e-mail shortly before the loan period ends. After that, you'll get another e-mail asking if you want to purchase the book, so you can take your time reading it.

Organizing your book selections

The Books library offers two different views (grid or list) and allows you to sort your books by author, title, or recent usage. You can also remove books from your Device library, which recovers storage space. Finally, you can remove books from your Amazon account completely if you never want to see them again.

To download books from your Cloud library:

1. Go to your Books Cloud library (Home screen > Books > Cloud).

2. Tap a book cover that doesn't have a check mark displayed on it. (The check mark means that book has already been downloaded to your device.)

3. The download progress is displayed on the cover . Tap the x button if you want to cancel the download.

4. A new banner appears on the cover, and the book is now listed in the Cloud library (with a check mark) as well as in the Device library **B**.

TIP Downloading a book requires an active Internet connection. The download will continue if you lose your connection in the middle of a download.

Ⓐ The download progress of a book is displayed here.

Ⓑ A newly downloaded book will sport a New badge.

G Tap the Menu icon to see the Books library view options, which display the current view. Tap to change.

D Three sorting options are available at the top of both the Cloud and Device libraries.

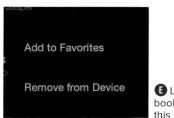

E Long tap a book to access this menu.

To switch views:

1. By default, your Books library is displayed as a grid of book covers (Grid View). Tap the Menu button.

2. Tap List View to change the view **G**.

3. Now, your books are displayed in a list. The cover is on the left; the name of the book and author are next to it **D**. The new badge is shown, as is the check mark denoting books on the device.

To sort your books:

1. Go to either your Cloud or Device Books library (Home screen > Books).

2. Under the Cloud and Device tab are the three sorting options available to you: By Author, By Recent, and By Title. The currently applied sort is displayed in orange. Tap one to apply the sort to your books.

TIP By Recent sorts your books in the order of most recently interacted with.

To remove a book from your Kindle Fire:

1. Go to your Books library (Home screen > Books).

2. Either switch to the Device library to see only books stored on your Kindle Fire or find a book with a check mark on it.

3. Long tap the book you want to remove **E**.

4. Tap Remove from Device, and the book is deleted from your Kindle Fire.

To delete a book from your library:

1. Deleting a book from your Kindle library permanently requires a visit to Amazon.com in the browser of your choice. Point your browser to amazon.com/manageyourkindle.

2. Log in with your Amazon account.

3. The contents of your Kindle library are listed **F**.

4. Click Books in the Your Kindle library navigation to list only the books in your Cloud library.

5. Find the book you want to delete and click the Actions menu **G**.

6. Click "Delete from library."

7. A confirmation appears asking if you really want to delete this book. All your notes and highlights will be deleted as well. Click Yes to delete the book from your Cloud library. The book won't show up on any of your Kindles or on Amazon.com. If you want to read the book later, you'll have to purchase it or borrow if from the library.

To return a borrowed book:

1. Log into Manage Your Kindle with your Amazon account.

2. Locate the borrowed book that you wish to return and click the Actions menu **H**. Books borrowed from your local library will have a digital library tag, while books from the Kindle Owners' Lending Library will display a Prime logo.

3. Click "Return this book." Click Yes in the Return Loan Confirmation window, and the book is returned. You will no longer be able to read this book, unless you purchase it or borrow it again.

F Your Kindle library in the Manage Your Kindle section of Amazon.com

> Read Now
> Deliver to my...
> Download & transfer via USB
> Clear furthest page read...
> Delete from library
> Loan this title

G The Actions menu on each book displays a number of different options, including "Delete from library."

> Read Now
> Deliver to my...
> Purchase this book
> Download & transfer via USB
> Clear furthest page read...
> Return this book

H If you want to return your library book ahead of schedule, click "Return this book."

TIP Library books are loaned to you for a limited time. At the end of that period, they are returned automatically. Books borrowed from the Kindle Owners' Lending Library have no due date, so you must return them manually before you can take out another book.

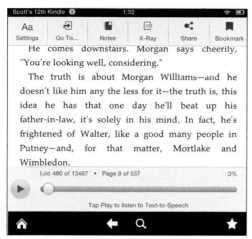

A The reading toolbar gives you access to a number of options.

Reading books

People have been reading books printed on paper for hundreds of years. Many credit the Kindle platform for the huge uptick in reading novels and other books on a variety of screens. Your Kindle Fire makes for a fantastic reading device thanks to the bright, vibrant screen and its relatively light weight. Best of all, you have access to thousands of books at your fingertips.

You can read books on your Kindle, and your device has two ways of reading them to you: Text-to-Speech and Immersion. Both are covered in this section.

To start reading a book:

1. Locate the book you want to read, either on the Carousel or in your Books library (Home screen > Books).

2. Tap the book. If it is on your device, the book opens, and you can start reading. If the book is in your Cloud library, the first tap downloads it (assuming you have an Internet connection). Tap once more to open the book and start reading it.

To access the reading toolbar:

1. Open a book.

2. Tap in the middle of a page, and the reading toolbar appear **A**.

To turn pages:

1. Open a book you want to read.

2. Tap the right side of the screen to page forward. Tap the left to page back. Your current location in the book is displayed on the lower-left corner, and the per-cent read is in the right corner 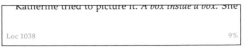.

3. To skim pages, tap to access the reading toolbar, and then slide the page slider back and forth **C**. As you slide, the pages change, and your current location (or page, if the book supports Real Page Numbers) is displayed. Lift your finger off the slider to read the page you're on.

TIP You can also swipe from right to left to page forward, and from left to right to go back, but tapping requires less finger movement.

B Your current location and the percentage of pages read are displayed at the bottom of the screen while you're reading.

C The page slider lets you jump to another point in the book quickly.

Locations and Real Page Numbers

Locations are like page numbers, except they are more granular. Each word in a Kindle book has a specific location in the book, designated with a number. This is the number displayed in the lower-left corner of the screen as you read a Kindle book.

Amazon has also introduced *Real Page Numbers* to some of their titles. They map the page numbering from a printed edition of a book to the Kindle version. If a book has Real Page Numbers, tapping the screen to bring up the controls will display your current page as well.

Aa Settings | Go To... | Notes | X-Ray | Share

D Settings determine the font size, color mode, margins, and font of a book. You can also turn on and off Text-to-Speech (where supported).

The Big Short: Inside the Doomsday M.
Lewis, Michael
You have read 1% of the book

Go to Page or Location

Sync to Furthest Page Read

Dedication

Epigraph

Contents

Prologue Poltergeist

Chapter 1 A Secret Origin Story   1

E The table of contents for a Kindle book

Enter page (1-266) or location (1-4240)

You are currently at page , location 31.

Cancel | Page | Location

F Enter a page number or location to zip right there.

To change the look of the book:

1. Open the reading toolbar.

2. Tap Settings **D**.

3. To increase the font size, tap the font icon that you want (10 is the largest). Tap the left icon to decrease the font size (1 is the smallest). Color mode changes both the color of the text and the background. Margins can be Narrow (the default), Normal, or Wide if you tap any of those buttons. You can change the font by tapping Font and picking from the list. Finally, you can turn on and off Text-to-Speech if the book supports this feature.

As you make changes, they are applied to the book, so you can decide if you like the font/color mode combination. If you're happy with the settings, tap anywhere other than the Settings menu to close it.

TIP These settings are not applied per book, but for the entire library.

To jump to a certain page or location in the book:

1. Bring up the reading toolbar.

2. Tap the Go To... button.

3. This lists the table of contents **E**. You can jump to a chapter by tapping it. Scroll down to see information about the author in some books.

4. Tap the Go to Page or Location button **F**.

5. Enter the page or location that you want to go to and tap either the Page or Location button.

TIP You can reset your place in WhisperSync on a per-book basis via **Manage Your Kindle** on Amazon.com. Click the Actions menu for the book you want to reset, and then click "Clear furthest page read."

To sync your place in a book manually with WhisperSync:

1. *WhisperSync*, an Amazon technology, saves your current place in a book across devices at certain intervals. Whenever you open a Kindle book, you'll almost always be on the page where you left off. Bring the reading toolbar onto the screen.

2. Tap Go To....

3. Tap the Sync to Furthest Page Read.

4. This forces your Fire to check with Amazon to see if you've read any further in this book on another device. Tap OK .

To zoom in on images:

1. Open a book with images in it.

2. Double tap with your finger on the image, and the image zooms to full screen 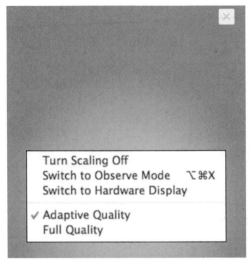.

3. Tap the x to exit the image.

TIP You can also long tap the image and tap Zoom from the menu.

To have your Kindle Fire read your books to you aloud:

1. Some books offer a *Text-to-Speech* feature, which uses a computer-generated voice to read the text of the book to you. Tap to bring up the reading toolbar and then tap Settings.

2. Tap On next to Text-to-Speech to enable it on books that include the feature .

3. Tap anywhere else on the screen to close Settings and then tap again to bring the reading toolbar on screen.

G You can check to see if you're at the most recently read page of your book.

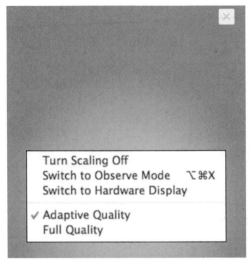

H A zoomed-in image. Tap the x to close it.

I The Text-to-Speech toggle

J When Text-to-Speech is enabled, a Play button appears in the book controls.

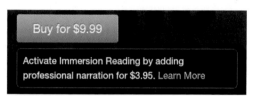

K The playback speed is controlled by the square button on the right.

L When professional narration is available, you can add it to a Kindle book for a fee.

M The "Add Narration for" button.

> ▶ ━━━━━●━━━━━━━━
> Tap Play to read with professional narration

N After the narration is added, the Play button will start the professional narration.

> **I. The Period**
>
> It was the best of times,
> it was the worst of times,
> it was the age of wisdom,

O As the narration unfolds, the text being read is highlighted.

> ↻ ◀)) ☀ 📶 ⟳ ⊕
> Unlocked Volume Brightness Wireless Sync More...
> 🔄30 ❚❚ 🔖 A Tale of Two Cities (Unabridged)
>   By Charles Dickens / Narrated by Simon...

P Controls appear in the Quick Settings screen so you can start and stop even when you aren't in the book.

4. A Play button appears next to the location slider **J**. Tap Play, and the Kindle will start reading from the top of the page. As it reads, the pages will turn themselves.

5. As Text-to-Speech is playing, a speed control appears **K**. Tap it to cycle through the options: 1x, 1.5x, 2x, 3x, 4x, and .7x.

6. Tap the Pause button to stop Text-to-Speech.

To use Immersion reading:

1. If a book in the Kindle Store (Home screen > Books > Store) has a professionally narrated version available, a notice is displayed on the book's page **L**.

TIP If you already own the book, you can add narration (when available) for an additional price **M**.

2. Tap the "Add Narration for" button, and the narration track is downloaded to your Kindle Fire as an audiobook (see Chapter 11).

3. Open the book and tap the screen to bring up the reading toolbar.

4. The note below the location slider now reads "Tap Play to read with professional narration." Tap Play **N**.

5. The narration starts on the page you're currently viewing, and the passage being read is highlighted **O**.

6. You can leave the book and the narration continues, unlike Text-to-Speech. Swipe down to access the controls for the narration. They are just like the controls for an audiobook (see Chapter 11) **P**.

7. Tap the Pause button to stop the narration.

Implementing bookmarks, highlights, notes, and definitions

Some features that are closely associated with reading physical books have survived the leap to ebooks: bookmarks, highlighting, and writing notes in the margins. The Kindle Fire allows you to do all these things with your Kindle books. You can even look up unfamiliar words in a book without having to leave the story.

To bookmark a page:

1. Open a book.

2. Turn to a page that you'd like to bookmark.

3. Tap the middle of the screen to bring up the reading toolbar.

4. Tap Bookmark, and the icon turns blue .

5. A bookmark icon appears on the book-marked page **B**.

TIP You can also bookmark a page by simply tapping its upper-right corner. The blue bookmark appears.

6. To remove a bookmark, tap it.

Bookmark

A The Bookmark button

> A TALE OF TWO CITIES
>
> ople in a dark room, watching and
> ning, always do.

B A bookmarked page

C As you select text, a magnifier lets you see a little better.

D Tap Highlight in the menu.

"Is it not impressive, Mr. Darnay?" asked Lucie. "Sometimes, I have sat here of an evening, until I have fancied—but even the shade of a foolish fancy makes me shudder to-night, when all is so black and solemn—"

E Text is highlighted in yellow.

F Typing a note

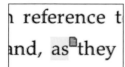

G The Note icon appears, and the selected text is also highlighted.

Page 63 - Note

This is a note.

Close   Delete   Edit

H Tap the icon to read the note. Tap Delete to get rid of it and Edit to change it.

To highlight text:

1. Open a book.

2. Find a word, sentence, or passage you'd like to highlight.

3. Tap the first word you want to include in the highlight. Blue highlighting appears, signifying that the word has been selected; a magnifier appears to help you see the words you're selecting **C**. With your finger still pressed against the screen, move down the screen until all the words you want are included in the highlighting.

TIP You can refine your selection by using the gray handles that bracket the selected text. Tap and drag on either handle to increase or decrease the amount of text selected.

4. Once you have selected all the text you want highlighted, tap Highlight on the menu that appears **D**.

5. The text is now highlighted in yellow **E**.

To create a note:

1. Open a book.

2. Find the passage or word where you'd like to place a note.

3. Tap the text to select it.

4. From the menu that appears, tap Note **D**.

5. Type your note in the Notes field **F**. Tap Save.

6. The text is highlighted, and a Note icon appears next to it **G**.

7. Tap the Note icon to read the note inline **H**. Close to exit the note.

To look up a word:

1. Open a book.

2. Long tap the word you are unfamiliar with, and the definition appears  ⓘ.

3. Tap Full Definition to read the full text of the definition ⓙ.

4. Tap the screen to bring up the reading toolbar, and tap the Back arrow to return to your book.

TIP Tap More in the pop-up menu for a couple of additional lookup options: Search in Book, Wikipedia, and the Web. In-book search is covered in the Search section. Tapping Search Wikipedia will take you to that word's Wikipedia entry. Tapping Search the Web does a Web search via your default search engine.

complete word, DIG. The floor was examined very

ex·claim /ik'sklām/ v. [*intrans.*] [often with *direct speech*] cry out suddenly, esp. in surprise, anger, or pain: *"Well, I never," she exclaimed; she looked in the mirror, exclaiming in dismay at her appearance.*

Full Definition

| Note | Highlight | Share | More... |

"My father," exclaimed Lucie, "you are ill!"

ⓘ Tapping a word brings up part of the definition automatically.

THE NEW OXFORD AMERICAN DICTIONARY

ex·cla·ma·tion /ˌekskləˈmāSHən/ *n.* a sudden cry or remark, esp. expressing surprise, anger, or pain: *Meg gave an involuntary exclamation; an exclamation of*

ⓙ The full definition from *The New Oxford American Dictionary*, included with the Fire

Notes

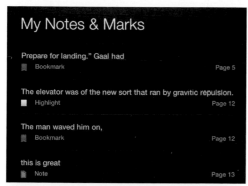

K The Notes button

My Notes & Marks lists all the notes, highlights, and bookmarks you've made in a book.

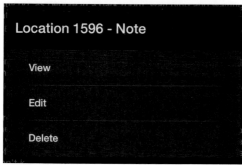

L My Notes & Marks lists all the notes, highlights, and bookmarks you've made in a book.

M Long tap a note to access this menu.

To manage all your notes, highlights, and bookmarks:

1. All of your notes, highlights, and book-marks are stored with your book and will *sync* across devices—open the same book on another Kindle, and they will all be there. Open a book and tap the screen to bring up the reading toolbar.

2. Tap the Notes icon **K**.

3. My Notes & Marks is the central loca-tion for you to access all your notes, highlights, and bookmarks in a list **L**. Each entry lists its type (Note, Highlight, or Bookmark); some text (the text of the note, the highlighted text, or the first few words of the bookmarked page); and the page or Kindle location on which it can be found.

4. Tap a note, highlight, or bookmark to jump to that location in the book.

5. Long tap a note, highlight, or bookmark and tap Delete to get rid of an entry **M**. Long tapping a note allows you to edit it.

Sharing books with others

Sharing means a few things in the Kindle book world: it refers to passages and quotes from books on social networks (Facebook and Twitter) and also loaning Kindle books to someone else (assuming this is permitted). This section covers how to connect your Kindle Fire to your social networks, sharing from within a book, and sharing a book with someone you know.

To set up your sharing accounts:

1. Swipe down from the top of your Kindle Fire to access Quick Settings.

2. Tap More > My Account  **A**.

3. Tap Manage Social Network Accounts to add or modify a Twitter or Facebook account **B**.

4. Tap either Facebook or Twitter to link your account.

5. Log in with the Facebook/Twitter account you want to link, and allow your Kindle Fire access to post on either of those networks.

6. Repeat until both your Twitter and Facebook accounts are linked to your Kindle Fire **C**.

TIP You can link only one Facebook and one Twitter account to your Kindle Fire.

To share on Twitter and Facebook:

1. Open a book that contains something you want to tweet.

2. Select the text by tapping and dragging it until it is all selected.

3. Tap Share **D**.

A My Account houses your social network accounts.

B At present, Facebook and Twitter are the only social networking accounts you can link to your Kindle Fire.

C When you link an account on your Fire, it is linked to your Amazon account.

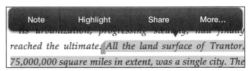

D Tap Share to post to Twitter or Facebook.

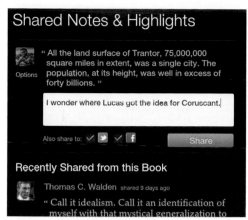

E Enter some text to post, check Twitter/Facebook, and tap Share.

F A link, along with your text, is posted to each social network.

G The quote and your text are also posted to http://kindle.amazon.com.

4. Shared Notes & Highlights opens **E**. At the top is the quote you selected with a section for an optional comment below. By default, your Twitter and Facebook accounts are selected. If you want to share only one, tap the other to uncheck it.

Under the Share box is a list of passages from the book that other Kindle readers have shared recently.

5. Tap the Share button. The selected quote is displayed at the top of the shared passages. It is also posted to Twitter, Facebook, or both, depending on your settings **F**. The text that you selected isn't posted to Facebook or Twitter directly. A link to http://kindle.amazon.com is posted; it has the full text as well as a link to purchase the Kindle book for those interested **G**.

TIP You can log into http://kindle.amazon.com with your Amazon account. Then, you can fill out your Kindle profile, follow people, and see what others are sharing and highlighting in popular books.

To lend a book:

1. Go to Manage Your Kindle on Amazon.com (www.amazon.com/manageyourkindle).

2. Enter your Amazon account information.

3. Click Books under Your Kindle library to view all your Kindle books.

4. Click the Actions menu next to a book to see if it can be loaned. If that is the case, "Loan this title" is an available action .

5. Click "Loan this title." Then, fill out the "Loan this book" form. Include the e-mail address of the borrower and, optionally, their name and a personal message ❶.

6. Click "Send now," and an e-mail is sent to the borrower. While the book is on loan, you can't read it on your Kindle Fire (or any Kindles for that matter) ❶. The borrower has seven days to accept the loan. If they fail to do so, the book is once again available for you to read. The borrower has a set number of days to read the book once they've accepted it. The publisher determines the length of the loan. At the end of that time, the book is returned to your library, and you can read it once more.

❶ Click "Loan this title" in the Actions menu of an item in your Kindle library on Amazon.com to lend a book to a friend.

❶ Enter the e-mail address of the borrower, along with an optional message.

Title Not Available

This title cannot be downloaded because it is currently on loan.

Cancel   Purchase

❶ You cannot open books borrowed by others on your Kindle Fire until they've been returned.

Search Results
Searching for "thursday"

Also by Jasper Fforde

...Also by Jasper Fforde SHADES OF GREY The Thursday Next Series ONE OF OUR THURSDAYS IS MISSING FIRST AMONG
Location 2

...SHADES OF GREY The Thursday Next Series ONE OF OUR THURSDAYS IS MISSING FIRST AMONG SEQUELS SOMETHING
Location 2

...BEAR "I think it's an episode of The Dukes of Hazzard." THURSDAY NEXT IN The Woman Who Died a Lot NOW WITH
Location 13

Ⓐ Search results for books highlight the search term and include some surrounding text for context.

Searching books and using X-Ray

Unified Search (see Chapter 3) allows you to search your Books library by title and author. This is useful, but it doesn't search the text of a book. *Book search*, however, does just that. You can search the complete text of any book on your Kindle Fire, as long as you've downloaded it to the device.

In addition to traditional search, some Kindle books have a feature called *X-Ray* that pulls out all the characters, locations, and central terms across the book and indexes them. Amazon bills it as "seeing the bones" of your book.

To search within a book:

1. Open a book you want to search.

2. Tap the screen to bring up the reading toolbar and tap the Search icon 🔍.

3. Enter your search term. Notice that Auto-suggest isn't available here; only the term you enter will be searched.

4. Tap Go on the keyboard and wait a few moments while the book is searched.

5. The search results show you how many times the term was found. Each instance is grouped within the section of the book where it appears (Chapter 1, and so on Ⓐ. The search term is highlighted in blue with some surrounding text displayed for context. The page number/location is shown at the bottom of each result.

6. Tap a result to go to that location in the book. Tap the Back button to return to your search results.

TIP If you want to search the whole book for a particular word or phrase on the current page, long tap, tap More from the menu, and then tap "Search book."

Using X-Ray

X-Ray is a specialized search available only in certain books. Amazon staffers compile all the instances of characters, locations, and terms in a book and create an "index." They annotate the index with information from Shelfari (www.shelfari.com), Amazon's social network for readers, and Wikipedia, the crowd-sourced encyclopedia.

To determine whether your book supports X-Ray:

1. Go to Amazon.com and search for the book that interests you.

2. Scroll down to the Product Details section.

3. X-Ray is listed here. If it is available for this book, it will say Enabled **B**.

TIP When you're on the product page of a book you own on your Kindle Fire, it will have an "X-Ray this book" section if the book is X-Ray enabled **C**. On the Kindle Fire's native Kindle Store, you can't tell if a book you haven't purchased is X-Ray enabled before you buy it.

To use X-Ray:

1. Open an X-Ray enabled book.

2. Go to a page where the characters/location/term that interests you is mentioned.

3. Tap the screen to bring up the reading toolbar.

4. Tap the X-Ray icon **D**.

5. This is the X-Ray screen **E**. At the top are three tabs that define the scope of your X-Ray options: Page, Chapter, and Book. By default, Page is shown, but to use X-Ray on the current chapter or the whole book, tap one of those tabs.

Text-to-Speech: Enabled ☑
X-Ray: Enabled ☑
Amazon Best Sellers Rank:

B Not all books are X-Ray enabled, so make sure you check the product details on Amazon.com.

C X-Ray this book appears as a new section when visiting an X-Ray enabled book that you own in the Kindle Store.

X-Ray

D The X-Ray icon on the reading controls

E The X-Ray of a book is divided into three tabs: Page, Chapter, and Book.

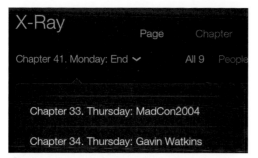

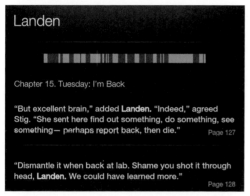

F The Chapter tab allows you to jump from one chapter to another.

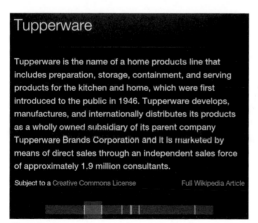

G All the X-Ray items for a character in a book

H X-Ray results for items sometimes include descriptions from Wikipedia.

Below those tabs are the subsections within the selected tab. You can filter X-Ray results to see only people or terms (with the number of occurrences listed next to it) by tapping one of the options. Tap All to display everything. The Chapter tab also includes a chapter drop-down so you can quickly apply X-Ray to other chapters **F**.

Next, the X-Ray entries (characters, locations, and terms) will yield different results, depending on the book. However, characters and terms are pretty common). Swipe to scroll through the list. The bar next to the term represents the total book. Sections in bright blue represent text in which the term is referenced or mentioned.

Then, tap one the entries to see some detail **G**. The term is displayed at the top of the screen with the bar of the book below. (In this case, the term is a character named *Landen*.) Because the scope of this X-Ray operation is Book, all the instances of the character are listed by chapter. The term is displayed in bold with some surrounding text to give you context. Tap any of the instances to jump to that point in the book. Tap the blue sections of the bar at the top to jump to a different point in the X-Ray of the term.

X-Ray often offers up some additional information about terms, locations, and sometimes characters as well **H**. This data is culled from Wikipedia, and it is displayed at the top of the page, above the bar representing the book.

Sideloading books

Generally, most people will add content to their Kindle Fires by purchasing it from one of Amazon's stores. Amazon takes care of delivering it to your device and syncing across devices, and it all works like magic. However, you can add content to your Kindle Fire yourself, without using any of Amazon's services. Loading content onto your Kindle this way is called *sideloading*. It involves connecting your Fire to a computer with a USB cable and transferring files into the device directly.

TIP **The Kindle Fire can be connected to a Windows PC without additional software. Connecting to a Mac for a USB transfer requires a special application.**

TIP **Sideloaded books will not sync their location, notes, bookmarks, or highlights across Kindles, nor will they be available in your Cloud library. Chapter 14 covers a way to load books and documents onto your Kindle and gain syncing.**

Supported file types

While you can transfer any kind of file you like to your Kindle Fire, it supports reading only certain file types. These are the file types that the Fire supports:

- AZW is a special Kindle format.
- MOBI is one of the original e-book formats, which is the basis for Amazon's AZW format.
- PDF is a common file type that mimics how a printed page looks.
- PRC is a format much like AZW.
- TXT is basic text.

All of these files will open just fine on your Kindle Fire, as long as they don't have any digital rights management (DRM) protection applied to them. The only DRM that your Fire supports is Amazon's own special flavor, which no one else uses.

A When you plug your Kindle Fire into a computer, this warning might appear.

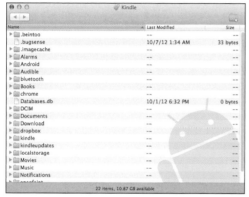

B The Android File Transfer application allows you to move files from your Mac to your Kindle Fire, and vice versa.

C The Kindle Fire is listed under Portable Devices when connected to a Windows 7 computer.

To connect your Kindle Fire to a Mac:

1. Locate a mini-USB to USB cable (one is included with your Kindle Fire).

2. Place the mini-USB side into your Kindle Fire and the other into a USB port on your Mac.

3. A USB compatibility message might appear **A**. If it does, tap OK on the alert. Then, go to http://kindle.com/support/downloads on your Mac. Follow the instructions to download and install the Android File Transfer app.

4. Once the app is installed, unplug and re-plug your Kindle Fire into a USB port on your Mac.

5. The Android File Transfer app launches automatically **B**. It lists all the folders and files on your Kindle Fire.

To connect your Kindle Fire to your PC:

1. Connect your Kindle Fire to your computer using a mini-USB to USB cable.

2. On Windows, the Kindle Fire will appear as a Portable Device or USB drive **C**.

3. Use Windows Explorer to browse the Kindle Fire's folders.

To load books from other sources onto your Fire via USB:

1. Connect your Kindle Fire to your computer using a mini-USB to USB cable.

2. Navigate to the Books directory via either Windows Explorer or the Android File Transfer app.

continues on next page

3. Drag the book you want to transfer to your Kindle Fire into the Books directory.

4. Wait for it to complete the copy.

5. The book is now on your Kindle Fire. Disconnect the Fire from your computer. The book will show up in your Docs library (see Chapter 14 for more information).

To load books from Amazon.com onto your Kindle Fire via USB:

1. Point your browser to Manage Your Kindle (www.amazon.com/myk/) and log in with your Amazon user name and password.

2. Your Kindle library is displayed. Next to each Kindle book you'll find an Actions button. Click the Actions button for the book you want to download and select Download & Transfer via USB .

3. In the drop-down list, select the Kindle that will receive the file you want to transfer. Then, click Download **E**.

4. Save the file somewhere on your computer where you will find it later.

5. Connect your Kindle Fire to a USB port on your computer using a mini-USB to USB cable. The Kindle will appear as a drive on your computer (Windows), or the Android File Transfer app will open (Mac).

6. Drag the book file you downloaded into the Books folder on your Kindle Fire.

7. Disconnect the Fire from your computer, and the book now appears in your on-device Books library.

D Access Kindle books on your computer by clicking Download & transfer via USB.

> Deliver to my...
> Download & transfer via USB
> Clear furthest page read...
> Delete from library

Download and transfer via USB

The Hydrogen Sonata
Banks, Iain M.

Which Kindle will you transfer this to?

Scott's 10th Kindle

Transfer Tip: After downloading, use your USB cable to connect your computer and Kindle. Your Kindle will appear as a drive on your computer. Copy your downloaded file from your computer to your Kindle's documents folder.

Download   Cancel

E Select which of your Kindles should receive the transferred book and click Download.

8

Music

The Kindle Fire is a great music player, though it won't fit in your pocket. The HD models sport Dolby speakers that sound surprisingly good for a device so small. In addition, all Kindle Fires have a headphone jack, so you can listen to your music whenever and wherever you find yourself.

Your Kindle Fire can do everything you expect from a music player: create playlists, purchase music, and browse your library for music.

This chapter covers purchasing music, downloading it, listening, managing your library, and using Amazon Cloud Player.

In this chapter

Buying music

Amazon.com offers a wide variety of music for purchase via the Kindle Fire. All of the digital music that Amazon sells is DRM-free and in MP3 format.

Every MP3 you purchase from Amazon is added to your Amazon Cloud Player automatically. The Cloud Player is, as the name suggests, a place in the *cloud* (on Amazon's servers) where your purchases are stored.

To buy on your Kindle Fire:

1. Tap Music on the Home screen.

2. Tap Store **A**. The Music Store front page has a few sections: At the top is a Search box. Below that, you'll find a variety of songs and albums that Amazon is promoting. Then, there is a selection of new releases and buttons to three categories: Bestsellers, New Releases, and Genres. A Recommended For You section lists things you might like, and at the bottom is another promotional area.

    Albums on the front page are displayed with their cover, their title, the name of the artist, the average rating, and a tappable button displaying the price.

    Songs display their album art, title of the song, name of the artist, a "Play sample" button, and a price button. Tap the "Play sample" button to hear a 30-second preview of the song. Tap again to stop the sample **B**.

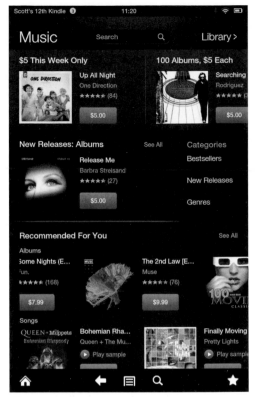

A The Music Store on your Kindle Fire gives you access to thousands of songs.

B Tap the Play button to hear a 30-second preview.

C When you tap the price button, it becomes a green Buy button.

D After completing a purchase, the music is added to your Cloud Player.

E As you type a search term, suggestions appear.

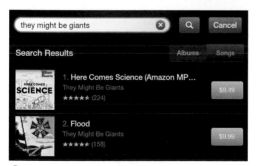

F The Search Results section has two tabs: Albums and Songs.

Tapping the price button on either an album or song turns it into a green Buy button **C**. Tap the Buy button, and the item is purchased, added to your Amazon Cloud Player, and becomes available in your library **D**. Tap "Go to your library" to listen to your music or tap "Continue shopping."

Tap the Search box to find something in particular. Search suggests some possible queries as you type. Tap one of the suggestions to search for it, or tap Return to search for exactly what you typed **E**.

The search results have two tabs: Albums (the default) and Songs. The Albums tab displays all the albums that meet your search criteria with their album art, name, artist name, and ratings displayed along with the price **F**.

continues on next page

The Songs tab displays the same information but includes a "Play sample" button for each song .

If you'd rather browse via categories, tap the Menu button and then Browse. This gives you the option of browsing New Releases, Bestsellers, or Genres **H**.

3. Tap an album/song to see the product detail **I**. Below the price is a link that'll take you to all the music by that artist in the store.

   The track listing has all the songs on the album with a Preview button on the left. When a track is available for individual purchase (which is most of the time), the price of the track is shown next to the name.

   Swipe up to look at Amazon's recommendations and read the reviews.

4. Tap the price button on the album or track you want to purchase.

5. Tap the green Buy button to purchase the item. It is added to your Amazon Cloud Player and available in the Cloud library on your Kindle.

G The search results for songs include a preview button.

H You can browse the Music Store by New Releases, Bestsellers, or Genres.

I View an album in the Music Store.

The Music Cloud library

Playlists display a collage of album art, the name of the playlist, and the number of songs.

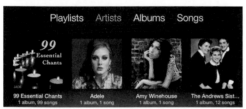

The Artists section of the Music library is organized by artist and displays how many albums and songs of each are in your library.

All of your albums are listed in a grid.

Listening to music

You can listen to music on your Kindle in a few ways: shuffling through your entire song collection, playing playlists or albums, or listening to all the songs by a particular artist.

To navigate your libraries:

1. Open your Music library (Home screen > Music).

2. At the top of the Music library are two tabs: Cloud and Device **A**. By default, you're in the Cloud library, which lists all the music you have in your Amazon Cloud Player. To play any of these songs, you'll need an active Internet connection. The Device library lists any music you've downloaded to your Kindle Fire.

   Each library is organized by Playlists, Artists, Albums, or Songs. The Playlists section displays all the playlists you've created with the name of the playlist, the number of songs, and a collage of the album art that composes the playlist **B**.

   Artists lists all the artists in your Music library. Some will display a picture, while others will be represented by an album cover. Under the cover/picture the name of the artist appears along with the number of albums and songs by that artist currently in your library **C**.

   Tap Albums to see a list of the albums in your library, along with the album art, the name, and the artist **D**.

   Songs displays all your songs in a list with album art, name of song and artist, and length **A**. Tap Shuffle at the top to start playing your entire music collection in random order (or at least those songs in the current library).

To play music:

1. Open your Music library (Home screen > Music).

2. If you want to play a particular album or playlist, tap the relevant section and find the album or playlist. If you want to play all the songs by an artist, tap Artists and then tap the artist you want to play. If you want to play a random song, tap Songs.

3. Whenever you're presented with a list of songs (a playlist, album, or list of songs by an artist), a Shuffle button appears at the top ❶. Tap Shuffle to play the list of songs in random order. If you want to play a particular song, just tap it.

4. The song loads, and the Now Playing screen is shown ❶. The album art is displayed with the name of the song below it. If the song's name is too long to fit on the screen, it will scroll automatically. The name of the album appears at the bottom.

TIP Long tap the cover art to add this song to a playlist, shop other songs by this artist, and more.

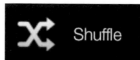

❶ The Shuffle button appears at the top of album, artist, and playlist listings.

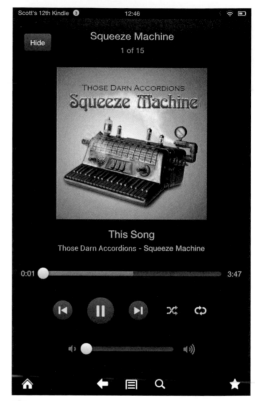

❶ When a song is playing, you can access the controls and see the cover of the album.

G The player has controls at the bottom of the Music library.

H Controls also appear below Quick Settings.

Below the information about the song is your current position in the song. Scrub forward or back by pressing your finger against the white button and dragging backward or forward.

The play controls are under the current location: Skip Back, Pause/Play, Skip Forward, Shuffle, and Loop. If Shuffle or Loop is active, it will be orange. Tap to play an album's songs in alphabetical order. Tap the Loop icon to play this list of songs over and over again.

Tap Hide to return to browsing your Music library. The currently playing song, along with play controls, is displayed at the bottom of the screen, and the music continues to play **G**.

You can also exit the Music library, and the music will continue to play. To access playback controls while you're outside the Music library, swipe down **H**. The name of the song, artist, and album name are displayed along with controls. Tap to pause/play and skip.

Downloading and deleting music

All the music in your Cloud library requires an active Internet connection in order to stream from Amazon's servers. The music in your Device library, however, can be listened to even when the device is in Airplane mode (with all networking shut down), though it takes up space on your Kindle Fire.

To download entire playlists, albums, or artists to your device:

1. All of your Amazon MP3 purchases are available in your Music Cloud library (Home screen > Music > Cloud). However, if you don't have an Internet connection, you'll want to download music to your Fire. Make sure you're in the Music Cloud library.

2. Go to the correct section of your Cloud library by tapping Playlist, Artists, or Album.

3. Tap the item you want to download and tap the "Download all" button **A**.

4. The tracks are added to the download queue, and the progress is displayed **B**. Once a track is downloaded to your device, a check mark is displayed above the time. The track is listed in your Device library as well as the Cloud library.

TIP Tap the x next to the download progress to cancel the entire download.

A A playlist in the Cloud library can be downloaded to the device.

B The download progress is displayed and can be cancelled by tapping the x button.

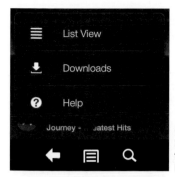

C Tap the Menu button to access Downloads.

D Monitor the progress of your downloads and see completed ones.

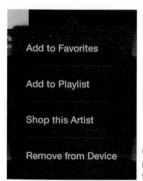

E Long tap to remove the album from the device.

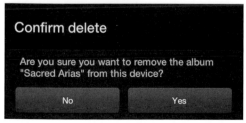

F Confirm the removal. If this is an album from your Cloud library, it will still be available in Cloud Player.

To monitor downloads, tap the Menu button and then tap Downloads **C**. You can watch as each track is downloaded and see if anything else is queued for download. Tap "See completed downloads" to display what's already been downloaded **D**.

5. Once the album/playlist/artist's songs have been downloaded to your device, they will display a check mark.

TIP Long tap an individual song and then tap "Download this song" to save it to your Kindle Fire.

To remove music from your Fire:

1. Go to your Device library in Music (Home screen > Music > Device).

2. Long tap the album or song you want to remove from the device **E**.

3. Tap Remove from Device.

4. Confirm that you want to remove the music from your device **F**.

   It is deleted. If this music is in your Cloud library, it will still be available there. You can re-download it later, but it is no longer taking up space on your device.

TIP To remove all downloaded music by a particular artist, go to the Artists section, long tap, and tap Remove All Songs by Artist from Device.

To delete music from your Cloud Player:

1. To delete a song or album from Cloud Player permanently, you must log into Cloud Player for Web on Amazon.com (Shop by Departments > MP3s & Cloud Player > Cloud Player for Web).

2. Click Songs under your music to find the song (or songs) you want to edit.

3. Hover over the song's name with your mouse and click the triangle to access the action menu **G**.

4. Click Delete.

5. This moves the item to the Deleted Items list, which you can access by clicking Deleted Items in the Your Music section **H**. The song will no longer show up in the Cloud library on your Kindle.

6. Click "Empty all deleted items" to remove the song permanently or "Restore all" to undelete.

TIP After you empty your deleted items, they are gone. If you want to listen to them later, you must purchase them again.

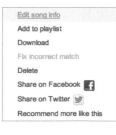

G The action menu on Cloud Player for the Web allows you to delete things permanently.

1 item was moved to Deleted Items list

H The item is moved to the Deleted Items list.

(A) All your playlists are grouped together.

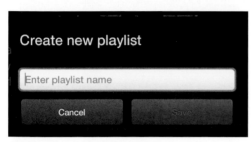

(B) Every playlist needs a name.

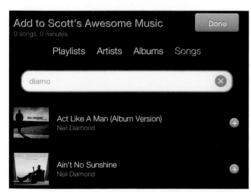

(C) Adding music to a playlist is as easy as tapping the + button.

Mastering playlists

Playlists are modern-day mix tapes. They allow you to create a list of unrelated songs that can be played back in whatever order you want (including randomly).

To create a playlist:

1. Open your Music library (Home screen > Music).

2. Tap Playlists in either library to see your current playlists (A). If you want to access this playlist on other devices, or via the Web, create it in your Cloud library.

   Even if you've never created a playlist on your Fire, there will be one or two waiting for you. The Cloud library contains two playlists that are created and updated automatically: Purchases includes every track and album that you've bought from Amazon, and Recently Added to Cloud lists any new tracks you've added to your Amazon Cloud Player.

   The Device library has one auto-populating playlist: Recently Added to Device.

3. Tap Create New Playlist.

4. Enter a name for your playlist and tap Save (B).

5. Now the fun part—adding music (C). You have to add music song by song, but you can browse your library using the same tabs: Playlists, Artists, Albums, and Songs. If you have a particular song in mind, you can also search for it. As you type your search phrase, results appear in real time.

continues on next page

6. Tap the orange plus (+) next to the song you want to add to your playlist. If you're browsing an album or playlist, tap the Add All button to include all the songs in your playlist at once 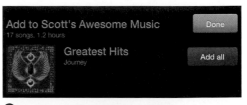.

The number of songs and play time of the playlist are updated under the name as you add music.

7. When you finish adding music, tap the Done button. The playlist is saved and opened.

To delete a playlist:

1. Go to your Music library (Home screen > Music).

2. Tap Playlists.

3. Long tap the playlist you want to delete .

4. Tap Delete Playlist from Cloud. If you're in your Device library, you will see Remove Playlist from Device.

5. Confirm that you want to delete this playlist by tapping Yes 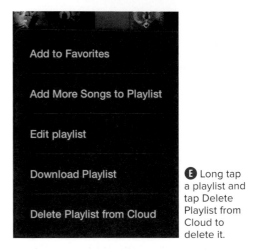. (Only the playlist is deleted; the music remains in your library.) The playlist is removed from the device and the cloud (if it was in your Cloud library).

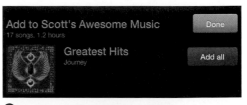

D It's easy to add entire albums by tapping "Add all."

E Long tap a playlist and tap Delete Playlist from Cloud to delete it.

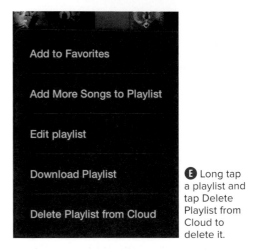

F Confirm your deletion. Keep in mind that the music on the playlist won't be deleted.

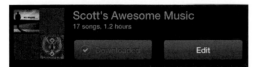

G Tap Shuffle to listen to this playlist on random.

H Tap Edit to add/remove music from a playlist.

[Playlist with songs shown]

I Tap and drag the handle to change the order of songs.

To play music from a playlist:

1. Go to your Music library (Home screen > Music).

2. Tap Playlists.

3. Tap the playlist you want to hear.

4. If you want to listen to the music in random order, tap Shuffle at the top of the playlist **G**. If you want to listen in order, tap the initial song. When the controls appear, make sure Shuffle is disabled 🔀.

To edit a playlist:

1. To remove a song from a playlist, you must edit it. Go into the playlist you want to edit (Home screen > Music > *library name* > Playlists).

2. Tap Edit **H**.

3. Now, you can remove any songs that are in the playlist by tapping the minus (–) sign next to it **I**. Add songs by tapping "Add songs" and selecting them. (Follow the instructions in "To create a playlist," earlier in this chapter.)

TIP Long tapping a song brings up a menu that includes "Add to playlist."

4. To rearrange the order of songs in your playlist, tap the handles next to the song you want to move, and drag the song into a new position. (The handles look like two rows of dots on the left side of the screen.)

5. Tap Done to save your changes.

Leveraging the cloud

Amazon Cloud Player stores all of your Amazon MP3 purchases for free on Amazon's servers. This allows you to play that music on your Kindle Fire anywhere you have a network connection. The basic level of service is free and comes with an additional perk: You can upload 250 songs from your personal music collection to your Cloud Player. These are songs you've purchased from elsewhere (probably iTunes) or ripped from CDs. You can upload them to your Cloud Player, and they then become available in the Cloud library on your Kindle Fire.

If you have an extensive collection of digital music that you didn't purchase from Amazon but you want to access it from your Kindle Fire, Cloud Player Premium is for you. Premium increases the number of imported songs from 250 to 250,000, which should be enough to cover most digital music collections.

To import music from your computer to Cloud Player:

1. Go to Amazon.com and click Cloud Player for Web under the MP3s & Cloud Player section of the Shop by Department menu. Log in.

2. Click the yellow "Import your music" button on Cloud Player for Web .

3. If you don't have the Amazon Music Importer, download it by clicking Download Now **B**. Follow the instructions to install it on your operating system.

4. Launch the Amazon Music Importer and click Authorize Device to allow the import from this computer **C**.

A Click the "Import your music" button to start the process.

B You must have the Amazon Music Importer. If you don't, download it.

C Authorize your computer to import music into the Cloud Player.

D The Amazon Music Importer will scan your computer for music, or you can point it to a particular folder.

E After the scan, you can import everything it found or select portions.

F Check the boxes next to the music you want to import.

5. The importer can scan your entire computer automatically looking for music to import, or you can manually tell it what to import **D**. The first time you run this, it is best to click Start Scan and allow it to look for the music.

6. Scan length will vary, but when complete, the importer displays how many songs it found on your machine. It then gives you the option to import all or select only certain songs **E**.

   If you click "Select music," you are able to choose folders, albums, and individual songs by checking the boxes next to them. When you're finished selecting songs, click "Import selected" **F**.

   continues on next page

7. The import progress is displayed with a "Pause import" button . The length of the import depends on the number of songs being imported and the speed of your Internet connection. The importer offers an estimated time remaining.

TIP **The import might be much quicker than you think because Amazon first checks to see whether it has a copy of the song you're importing. If it does, it just places its own copy of the song into your Cloud Player, so no upload is needed.**

8. All the songs have been imported into your Cloud Player, so click Close to quit the importer. The songs should be available in the Cloud library on your Kindle Fire in a few moments. They are all placed in the Recently Added to Cloud playlist.

G The import progress appears.

9

Videos

Watching video on your Kindle Fire is a great experience. The screen is bright, the size is just right, and the Kindle Fire HD can play back HD video so it looks super crisp. The Kindle Fire is very portable; you never have to sit in a doctor's office again without anything to do (or walk for hours on the treadmill staring at the wall).

In this chapter

Renting and purchasing video

Amazon's digital video offers come in three basic groups: Prime Instant Videos, rentals, and videos for purchase. Rental and purchased videos can be downloaded to your Fire and stored in your Videos library. Because they are saved to your device, you can watch downloaded videos at any time without an Internet connection.

Amazon stores your purchased videos on its servers, and you can re-download them at any point.

To purchase a TV show:

1. Go to the Videos library (Home screen > Videos).

2. You are taken to the Videos Store when you open the Videos library **A**. Like the other storefronts, there is a Search box at the top, some promoted movies and TV shows, and then a variety of sections highlighting different videos.

   To search the store, tap the Search box and start typing **B**. Suggestions appear; tap one to search for it, or tap the Search icon to search your entered query. The search results appear with a Refine button that lets you filter them **C**.

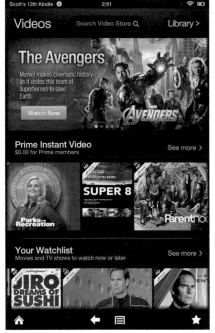

A The front page of the Videos Store

B As you type in the Search field, suggestions appear.

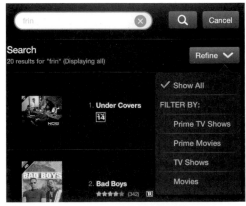

C Refine your search by filtering the results.

D The Movies and TV categories each have Prime and All tabs in addition to editor-created subsections.

E The product page of a TV show with several seasons

Amazon groups a number of videos to make it easier for you to browse them. The TV shows section, for example, is featured on the front page of the store. Tap "See more" to display a list of the shows available **D**.

There are two tabs at the top of the list: Prime and All. All is selected by default. It includes rental and purchase options, not just streaming videos. Below that is a menu you can swipe with different groups of TV shows (or movies), such as Popular TV Shows and Latest Episodes. Tap a name to list the shows.

3. Tap any TV show to see more information about it, including pricing **E**. The name and season of the show are displayed above the title art. Next to that are a few buttons: Buy the season in SD (with the price); Buy the season in HD; and Add to Watchlist (more on that in the "Watching video" section). A description of the show and a menu with all the available seasons rounds out the top section.

At the bottom of the listing are details about the season—most importantly if it is available in HD. You will also see shows that other people who like this one bought **F**.

continues on next page

F Details about the show, including whether it is available in HD

4. If you want to purchase an entire season, tap the orange price button (SD or HD). It turns into a green Buy button. Tap again to complete the purchase.

Once the purchase is complete, a green banner appears at the top of the entry indicating you own the season, and the Purchase buttons are removed **G**.

Tap a particular episode in a season list to access the Download and Streaming buttons **H**.

If you want to play this video without having to worry about having an Internet connection, download it to your device. Tap the Download button. If you've purchased the HD version, an alert will appear asking if you want to download the HD (better quality) or SD version (faster download) **I**. Tap which you prefer, and check the box to have it remember your selection.

TIP When downloading an SD video, a similar alert will appear asking if you want to download the best quality or the version that'll download fastest.

To purchase a single show, tap to see the purchasing options **J**. The Buy buttons function the same as for the seasons, except you're paying for only a single episode.

TIP A video that doesn't have a Prime marker on it  is generally available for download.

To purchase or rent a movie:

1. Go to the Videos library (Home screen > Videos).

2. Search for the movie that interests you, or tap "See more" in the Movies section to browse the entire collection.

G Purchased seasons display a green banner.

H The "show detail" section allows you to watch or download a specific episode.

I You can tap options for downloading HD or SD.

J Tap an episode to see purchasing options.

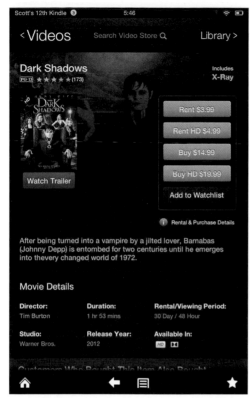

Scott's 12th Kindle 🔋   5:46   🔅 📶 🔋

< Videos   Search Video Store 🔍   Library >

Dark Shadows
PG-13 ★★★★★(173)   Includes
X-Ray

Rent $3.99

Rent HD $4.99

Buy $14.99

Buy HD $19.99

Watch Trailer

Add to Watchlist

ℹ️ Rental & Purchase Details

After being turned into a vampire by a jilted lover, Barnabas (Johnny Depp) is entombed for two centuries until he emerges into the very changed world of 1972.

Movie Details

Director:	**Duration:**	**Rental/Viewing Period:**
Tim Burton	1 hr 53 mins	30 Day / 48 Hour
Studio:	**Release Year:**	**Available In:**
Warner Bros.	2012	HD ▣

Customers Who Bought This Item Also Bought

🏠   ←   ☰   ★

Ⓚ A product page for a movie that can be rented or purchased

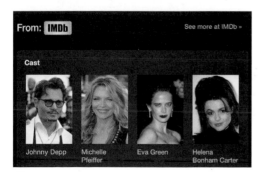

From: IMDb   See more at IMDb »

Cast

Johnny Depp   Michelle Pfeiffer   Eva Green   Helena Bonham Carter

Ⓛ IMDb information for the cast and crew of some movies is located at the bottom of their store pages.

3. Tap a movie that interests you Ⓚ. Movies don't have seasons and can be rented, so there are additional buttons in the purchase area.

At the top are the movie's name, rating, and average customer rating, with the movie poster and a Watch Trailer button below. Tap the Watch Trailer button to see the movie's trailer. If the movie supports X-Ray, an Includes X-Ray button will be shown. (See the task "To use X-Ray" for more information.) Movie details, including the cast and crew, release date, and the Rental/Viewing Period, are the final parts of the top section.

At the very bottom of the page, after the list of movies others have purchased and the reviews, is some information about the movie from IMDb.com (Internet Movie Database) Ⓛ. Tap any of the cast or crew to see more information about them and their other titles Ⓜ.

continues on next page

Chloë Grace Moretz   From: IMDb

Chloe Grace Moretz was born in Atlanta, Georgia, USA.

Chloe's first 2 appearances were as Violet in two episodes of The Guardian, on TV. Her first movie role was as Molly in Heart of the Beholder, a story about a family who opened the first video cassette store in

+ Read More

Known For

(500) Days of Summer (2009)   Let Me In (2010)

Hugo (2011)   Kick-Ass (2010)

Watch other titles with Chloë Grace Moretz

Ⓜ Tapping an actor brings up more information from IMDb, including a list of their other videos.

4. Tap either the SD or HD Purchase button to buy the movie. A green banner appears that says "You own this video," and the Buy buttons are replaced with a Watch Now button (for streaming) or a Download button .

If you just want to watch the movie once, renting is for you. Tap either of the Rental buttons, and it will turn into a green Rent button. Tap again, and you've rented the movie. A green banner lets you know you've rented the movie and exactly how long you have to watch it . You have 30 days to start watching most rentals. Once you start watching a rented video, you have 48 hours to finish it before losing access to it. You can always rent it again. The rental period information for each movie is listed in the Movie Details section.

TIP Some movies are available for rental *or* purchase. In those cases, only the relevant buttons will be displayed.

N A green banner displays when you visit a movie you own. Watch Now and Download buttons appear.

O Rental information is displayed at the top of a rented movie's product page.

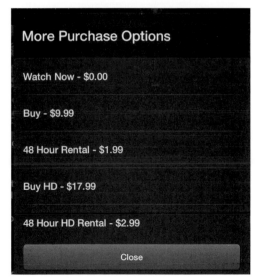

A The Prime logo lets you know this movie is available via Prime Instant Videos.

B A product page banner appears on Prime Instant Videos movies and shows.

C You can still purchase/rent movies and shows that are part of Prime Instant Videos.

Watching video

The general video controls are the same no matter what you're watching. This section covers watching Prime Instant Videos and videos in your library. It also explains how to hook up your Kindle Fire to an HDTV and watch video on it.

To stream Prime Instant Videos:

1. Prime Instant Videos is a service, much like Netflix, that is available to Amazon Prime members. The videos are free to stream for Prime members, and members can watch an unlimited amount of them.

   Tap "See more" in the Prime Instant Videos section of the Videos Store to see some of the videos that are included in the program.

   The Prime Instant Videos service is available across every section of the store. Each is designated with a Prime banner **A**.

2. Tap a video; both movies and TV shows are available **B**. The banner at the top notifies you that this video is included with your Prime membership. A Watch Now button appears where the purchase/rental buttons usually appear.

   You can still rent/purchase a Prime video if you want. Tap Purchase Options to see all the choices available to you **C**.

   TIP Streaming a Prime video requires an active Internet connection.

3. Tap the "Play now" button to start the video.

To watch a video from your library:

1. Any videos you purchase or rent from Amazon are listed in your Videos library (Home screen > Videos > Library) . It has two sections: Cloud and Device. They are further divided into two areas: Movies and TV.

   You can sort either library by tapping the Menu button and then the Sort By button **E**. There are two sort options: Recent or Title **F**. Make a choice, and your videos are sorted immediately.

D The Videos library on your Fire is divided into Cloud and Device and then further into Movies and TV.

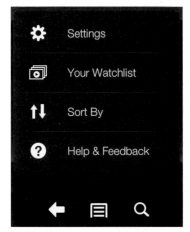

E Tap the Menu button to change the sorting options for the library.

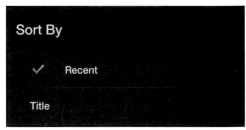

F You can sort either library by recent additions or title.

G Long tap a movie in the library to get this menu.

H Long tap a TV show to see these options.

2. Long tap a movie to bring up some watching options G. You can download the movie, view some details, or watch it right now.

Long tapping a TV series allows you to add it to your watchlist (more on that in a moment) or view season details H.

3. Tapping the View details button for either a movie or a TV show brings you to that video's page in the store. Tap the green Watch Now button on a movie or the Play button next to the TV episode to start watching.

To control a video that is playing:

1. Find a video and start watching it.

2. The video starts to play in landscape mode . Videos play in landscape or widescreen mode. If you rotate your Fire, the video will flip, still in landscape mode.

   The controls are displayed as the video starts to play . At the top right is the volume control. Tap and drag to increase or decrease volume; you can also use the hardware controls. Along the bottom of the screen are the Play controls.

   The Play/Pause button is on the lower-left corner. Above it is the 10-second rewind button. Tap it to rewind exactly 10 seconds in the video. Repeated tapping will rewind in 10-second increments. Next to the Play/Pause button is the video scrub bar; the name of the video is displayed above it. Press and drag your finger across the bar to jump to different sections of the video. If you're streaming, the scroll bar fills to reflect the amount of video cached.

   To the left of the scrub bar, the amount of the video you've watched is displayed with the total duration on the right.

   If the video you're watching is in HD, the HD icon will appear in blue. When watching a TV show, a Next Episode button is displayed. Tap it to watch the next episode in the series.

   The Back and Home buttons are also displayed.

3. Tap the screen to dismiss the controls. Tap again to bring them back.

① The video control's screenshots do not include the video that was playing.

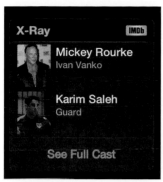

J The X-Ray menu in a movie

K Tapping an actor in X-Ray brings up an info pane about them.

L Tap Full Cast to see the entire cast. Tap a cast member to see more information about them.

To use X-Ray:

1. Start a video that includes the X-Ray feature; the video's product page will display the X-Ray icon.

2. While watching a scene, tap the screen to bring up the video controls **J**. In addition to the normal controls, X-Ray will appear in the upper-left corner. It lists all the actors in the current scene, along with a blue See Full Cast button.

   Tap an actor's entry to see their IMDb entry displayed over the video. The video pauses **K**. The actor's picture, movies, and biography are displayed. You will also see a list of movies/shows they appear in that are available in the Videos Store. Tap one to go to its product page. Tap the x to return to your video.

   Tapping the See Full Cast button brings up the head shots of all the actors in the movie and the roles they play **L**. Tap an actor to find out more information. Tap the x to return to your video.

To create a watchlist:

1. A *watchlist* is a queue of videos you want to view at some point. You can keep it on your Kindle Fire and add videos easily as you're browsing the store. Long tap a video and then tap Add to Watchlist.

   If you're on a video's product page, just tap the Add to Watchlist button **M**.

2. To access your watchlist, tap the Menu button and then Your Watchlist.

3. Your watchlist is divided into the same sections as your Videos libraries: Movies and TV and, within those sections, Prime and All **N**.

   You can add any videos (rentals, purchasable, and streaming only) to your watchlist.

   Tap any of your watchlist items to see the product information and the available watching options.

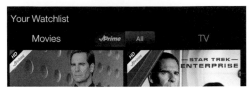

M The Add to Watchlist button appears on all videos in the store.

N Your watchlist is divided into Movies and TV and then Prime and All videos.

10

Newsstand

Newsstand gathers all your Kindle magazine and newspaper subscriptions. Here, you can read, subscribe to, and sample (with a trial subscription) a variety of newspapers and magazines. Traditionally, Kindle magazines and newspapers have been black-and-white affairs because of the limits of e-ink Kindles. The Kindle Fire, as you know, has a great color screen, and lots of magazines and newspapers now take advantage of this feature by offering their content in full color.

There are four kinds of periodicals in Newsstand: newspapers, magazines, magazines with Page View, and apps. This chapter will cover the differences and show you how to subscribe to magazines and newspapers.

In this chapter

Buying periodicals

The Newsstand Store looks and works very much like the other stores on your Kindle Fire 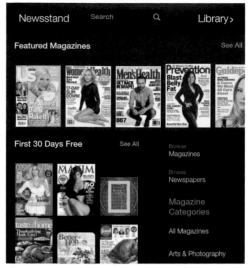. The front page shows a variety of magazines and newspapers for sale with featured periodicals at the top. The right side has a list of categories, and the rest of the page is taken up with various groupings of magazines and newspapers for purchase.

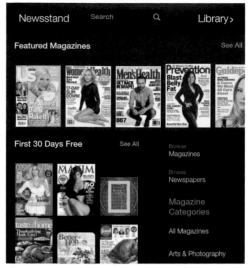

Ⓐ The Newsstand Store front page

Magazine types

Three types of magazines are available in the Newsstand Store:

- **Magazine:** By default, all magazines and newspapers in the Newsstand are in Text View. All the text of the articles and pictures are included. These magazines contain all the content of the issue but not the print layout.

- **Magazine, Page View enabled:** In addition to Text View, periodicals include faithful representations of their print counterparts. This is called *Page View*, which replicates the print experience in every way. So, you see high-resolution pictures of the magazine pages. In this view, magazine layout remains intact, but you can't do things such as change the font size of the text or tap to look up a word.

- **App:** Some publishers include videos and other interactive features in their magazines, which means they need custom magazine files. These magazines are delivered via apps that contain stores where you can purchase or subscribe to the magazine within the app. Apps are generally free to download, and they appear both in Newsstand and in the Apps library. Each app has a different interface, so they are not covered in this book.

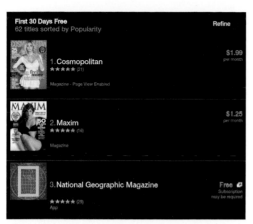

First 30 Days Free
62 titles sorted by Popularity   Refine

1. Cosmopolitan $1.99
★★★★★ (21)   per month
Magazine - Page View Enabled

2. Maxim $1.25
★★★★★ (16)   per month
Magazine

3. National Geographic Magazine   Free
★★★★★ (29)   Subscription
App   may be required

B A list of magazines available in the store. Notice that the magazine type is listed.

C A magazine's product page

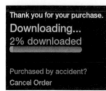

D The download progress of a magazine is displayed after you choose to subscribe or purchase an issue.

To purchase a newspaper or magazine:

1. Open the Newsstand Store (Home screen > Newsstand > Store).

2. Tap a section to see the periodicals listed within it, or search for a specific magazine or newspaper **B**. Either way, the results will look the same: magazine cover on the left, the price per month on the right. In between, you'll see the magazine's name, rating, and type.

3. Tap the magazine or newspaper subscription that interests you **C**. The product page has all the standard elements: the name of the periodical, the ratings, a description, and similar items in the store.

   When you subscribe to a magazine or newspaper, it is delivered to your Kindle automatically on a certain schedule. That schedule is displayed in the Delivered section (daily, weekly, or monthly are all examples of delivery schedules). Below that, you'll see a couple of prices: the subscription price and the price for the current issue of the periodical.

4. To subscribe to the periodical, tap the "Subscribe now" button **C**. This starts your free trial and downloads the current issue to your Kindle Fire. (The trial is usually 14 days, but the product page will specify the length.) After the trial ends, you're charged the subscription price. You can cancel before the trial is over and pay nothing. (See "Managing issues and subscriptions" for more information).

   Tap the Buy Issue button to purchase the current issue. As soon as you tap the button, the issue downloads. There is no confirmation, so be sure you want to purchase the issue before you tap **D**.

Reading periodicals

Your library is full of periodicals, and now it is time to get a cup of coffee and settle down for some reading. This section covers the basics of reading a magazine or newspaper, as well as switching from Page View to Text View (where supported).

To read a magazine:

1. Go to your Newsstand library (Home screen > Newsstand).

2. A grid of your magazines and newspapers is displayed in your Cloud library **A**. Those downloaded to your device have a check mark on their covers. Tap Device to see only those magazines on your device. Those recently delivered have a new banner on the cover.

   If you would rather see your periodicals in List View, tap the Menu button and then tap List View **B**.

3. Tap a magazine or newspaper to open it. If it isn't on your device, it must be downloaded before it can be opened.

   If you have more than one issue of a magazine or newspaper, the most recent issue's cover is displayed. Tap the cover to see a list of all the back issues **C**. Tap a back issue to download and open it.

A The Newsstand library

B The Newsstand library in List View

C Back issues of your periodicals are accessed by tapping the most recent issue in your library.

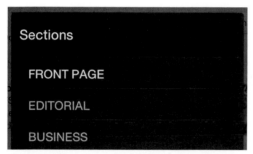

D A periodical, in this case a newspaper, in Text View

E The sections of the periodical; tapping a section jumps to it.

F The controls at the bottom of the screen

4. Magazines and newspapers in Text View open to a table of contents **D**. Tap the Sections drop-down at the top right of the screen to jump to different sections **E**.

Tap any of the stories to read them in full. Tap the right or left of the screen to turn the page forward or backward (you can also swipe either way).

Tap the screen to bring up the controls **F**. The number of pages in the article is displayed with arrows on either side. Tap one of the arrows to skip to the previous or next article.

In the navigation bar, you'll find these buttons: Back, Appearance (covered in "To change appearance in Text View"), Table of contents, Search, and Favorites.

TIP Tap a word to see its definition in Text View.

continues on next page

Magazines that support Page View open in that mode . When you turn the page, a page curl animation appears. Double tap a column of text or picture to zoom in on it. Double tap again to view the whole page.

TIP **You can turn off the page animation by bringing up the controls, tapping the appearance icon, and tapping Off** **.**

Turn your Kindle Fire to landscape mode, and you're able to see two pages of the magazine at once .

Tap the screen to bring up the controls . The thumbnails of the magazine appear. Swipe to page through the thumbnails; tap a page to jump to it.

G Page View of a magazine, with navigation shown at the bottom of the screen

H Turn the page curl animation on or off.

I When viewed in landscape mode, you can see two pages of a Page View magazine.

Strong, Silent Type

A leading manufacturer of electric trucks aims to recharge America's streets.

DAVID GOLDMAN / AP IMAGES FOR FRITO LAY

Plugging in: A Smith electric delivery van (in New York City) can reduce emissions by 85 percent, compared with diesel power.

JERRY ADLER | 559 words

When you press the accelerator of a Smith truck, it moves forward briskly, smoothly and in eerie quiet.

J The Text View of an article in a magazine that supports Page View

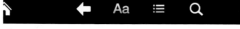

K The appearance options are available in Text View.

To switch from Page View to Text View:

1. Open a magazine that offers Page View.

2. Double tap some text to read it in Text View **J**.

3. Tap the screen to bring up the controls, and you'll see the familiar Text View controls. Tap the arrows to jump to other articles in Text View.

4. Tap the x to switch back to Page View.

TIP Tap the table of contents icon when in Text View to see a list of the articles in the magazine.

To change appearance in Text View:

1. Open an article or magazine in Text View.

2. Tap the screen to bring up the controls.

3. Tap the Appearance button **K**. You can change the font size by tapping the larger or smaller font icons. Color mode changes the text and background colors. You can also alter margins and choose different fonts.

To search in a magazine or newspaper:

1. Open the magazine or newspaper you want to search.

2. Tap the screen to bring up the controls and then tap the Search icon $\mathbf{Q}$.

3. Enter your search query and tap the Search icon.

4. The issue is searched, and the results are shown with the query text highlighted **L**. The results are grouped by article.

5. Tap a result to go to that part of the article.

Search Results

25 results for "food"

...Everyday Food Kindle Edition, 2012 © Martha Stewart Living Omnimedia, Inc. EDITOR'S LETTER cozy up! CON POULOS 187

EDITOR'S LETTER

...days: longer nights. Fall evenings are the perfect time to cook the food you crave all year and linger around the table. It's

...in my house! See my fun variations on page 45. I love comfort food as much as the next person (which is to say, a lot!), but

...want a little change of pace. That's why, for our annual Comfort Food issue, we transformed old favorites, like chicken parm, into

WHY DO WE CRAVE COMFORT FOOD?

...WHY DO WE CRAVE COMFORT FOOD? Here are three reasons why mac and cheese makes us feel better—and why salads and

L The search results

A Long tap a periodical in your library to bring up this menu.

B Your Kindle library lists your subscriptions with a blue label.

C The Actions menu contains the "Cancel subscription" action.

D When you cancel your subscription, you can include a reason or just cancel.

Managing issues and subscriptions

Once you've subscribed to a bunch of periodicals, you might want to cancel one or change which Kindle receives the subscription. You can't do this on your Kindle Fire directly; you have to go to Amazon.com.

To manage issues:

- By default, when a new issue of a periodical is delivered to your Kindle Fire, the older one is moved to your Cloud library and removed from the Device library. If you want to keep an issue on your device, long tap it in the library and then tap Keep **A**. If you ever want to remove this issue after that, you must do so manually.

- To remove an issue of a magazine or newspaper manually, long tap it in the library, and tap Remove from Device **A**.

To cancel a subscription:

1. Point your browser of choice to http://amazon.com/myk.

2. Log in with your Amazon.com account.

3. Your Kindle library is displayed with subscriptions noted in blue **B**.

4. Click the Actions menu next to the subscription you want to cancel and then click "Cancel subscription" **C**.

5. Provide some optional feedback about your cancellation, if you like, and click Cancel Subscription **D**.

   The subscription is cancelled, but you can still access any issues you received until your cancellation date.

To change delivery location:

1. Point your browser of choice to http://amazon.com/myk.

2. Log in with your Amazon.com account.

3. Click Subscription Settings under Your Kindle Account **E**.

4. All your subscriptions are listed here **F**. "Deliver future editions to" determines where the next issues of your subscription go. Click Edit next to the location of the magazine you'd like to change.

5. Select the Kindle that should receive future issues from the drop-down list **G**.

6. Click Update. The next issue will be sent to the Kindle that you indicated.

E Your Kindle Account includes a link to your subscription settings.

F All of your Kindle subscriptions can be edited here.

Deliver Future Editions   Close ⊠

Deliver To: Scott's 12th Kindle   ⬍

Update   Cancel

G Select the Kindle that should receive the latest issues of this subscription.

Audiobooks

Audiobooks are professionally read books that you can listen to on your Kindle Fire. Amazon owns a company called Audible.com, which is devoted solely to selling audiobooks. If you have an Audible.com account, you can link your Kindle Fire to it and enjoy your audiobooks on the device.

If you don't have an Audible.com account, you can still purchase and listen to audiobooks on your Kindle Fire.

In this chapter

Purchasing audiobooks

There are two ways to purchase audiobooks for your Kindle Fire: going to the Audiobooks Store on your Fire or using an Audible.com account. This chapter will cover how to use the Audiobooks Store on your Fire whether or not you have an Audible.com account.

TIP You can find more information about Audible accounts at Audible.com, including plans and rates.

To buy an audiobook from the Audiobooks Store:

1. Open the Audiobooks Store (Home screen > Audiobooks > Store) **A**. The front page lists a number of highlighted audiobooks for sale, their names, the name of the author, and the name of the narrator. Tap Play Sample to hear a sample of the book.

   Along the right side is a list of categories and features that you can browse by tapping them.

   Search the Store by tapping in the Search box at the top of the screen and entering your search terms. All search results and category listings can be refined by tapping the Refine button, which lets you sort and filter **B**.

   Tap the Menu button, no matter where you are in the store, to access the Storefront, Best Sellers, and New & Noteworthy list **C**.

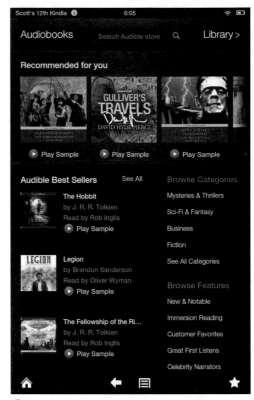

A The front page of the Audiobooks Store

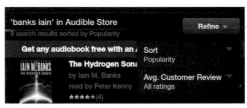

B Search results and categories can be refined by sorting and filtering.

C The Menu button gives you access to the Storefront, Best Sellers, and New & Noteworthy list.

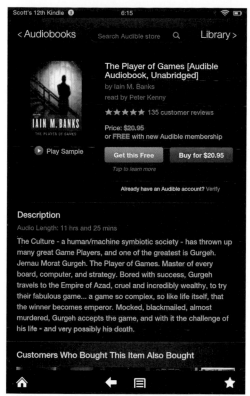

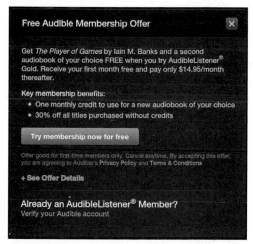

2. Tap an audiobook to see its product page **D**. The cover of the audiobook is displayed with a Play Sample button under it. Customer reviews are shown above the two Price buttons. The duration of the audiobook is listed at the top of the description, with related books and reviews underneath.

If you haven't linked your Audible.com account to this Kindle Fire, a Get this Free button will be displayed. Tap it and an alert appears explaining that in order to get this audiobook for free, you must sign up for an Audible.com account **E**. Tap "Sign up," and you are signed up for a trial account with the e-mail address and payment information associated with your Amazon account. If you have an Audible.com account already, verify it by tapping Verify your Audible.com account and entering the information requested.

continues on next page

D An audiobook's product page lists the price and description of the audiobook among other things.

E Sign up for an Audible.com membership and get a free audiobook.

You're returned to the product page, and now there is a green Listen Now button **F**.

If you don't want to sign up for Audible.com, simply tap the Price button to purchase the audiobook. A green Play Now button appears.

TIP An Audible.com account gives you credits for each book you can listen to according to your account level. When you visit an audiobook's product page and your Audile account is linked to your Kindle Fire, a credit button appears along with a discounted price **G**.

3. The audiobook appears in your Audiobooks Cloud library, though it must be downloaded before you can listen to it.

TIP After 30 days, you'll be charged for your Audible.com membership. Go to Audible.com and sign in with your Amazon account to modify all your Audible.com account settings, including cancelling the account.

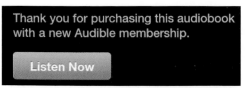

F After you purchase an audiobook, a Listen Now button appears.

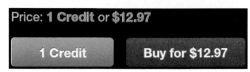

G Audible.com members get special pricing and can pay for audiobooks with credits.

(A) The Audiobooks Cloud library

(B) List View gives you more information at a glance.

(C) You can play an audiobook before it downloads completely. Tap the Play button.

Listening to audiobooks

Audiobooks can be played through your Kindle Fire's speakers or listened to via headphones. The controls are very much like the music playback controls with a few changes. This section covers listening to audiobooks, creating notes and book-marks, and editing them.

To listen to an audiobook:

1. Go to your Audiobooks library (Home screen > Audiobooks).

2. The Cloud library contains all the audiobooks you've purchased from Amazon (A). Tap the Menu button and then List View to see some more information about each audiobook, including the length and how much time is remaining (B). Tap the Menu button again and then tap Grid View to switch back to Grid View.

> **TIP** A check mark means that audiobook has been downloaded to your device.

Along the top of the library are the four sorting options. Tap one to sort by it.

3. Tap the audiobook you'd like to listen to (C). If it isn't already on your device, the download progress will be dis-played. A Play button will appear when enough of the audiobook has been downloaded for you to listen to it. Tap it to play.

continues on next page

4. The play controls appear with the cover image in the center **D**. Above the cover is a slider. Tap and drag your finger forward and back to scrub through the audiobook. The current chapter is displayed, as is your place in the book and the amount of time remaining.

If you want to skip to another chapter, tap the Index button at the top-right corner **E**. Tap the chapter you want to listen to, and you'll jump there.

Below the cover image is some information about the book and the play controls. Tap the Pause button to stop the audiobook; tap again to resume playing. The 30-second rewind allows you to jump back 30 seconds in the book; repeated taps jump again and again.

Next to the play controls is the speed controller. Tap the Rabbit icon to play the audiobook faster (1.5x, 2x, and 3x faster than normal). Tap the Turtle icon to slow it back down to a minimum of 0.5x speed.

The volume control at the bottom of the screen will increase or decrease the volume of the audiobook.

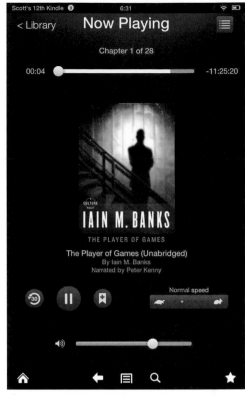

D The audiobook player controls

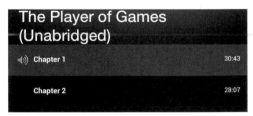

E The table of contents lets you jump from one chapter to another.

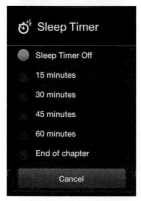

F The Menu button includes the Sleep Timer button.

G The sleep timer will stop playback automatically after a set period.

H Tap the Bookmark icon to bookmark a specific time.

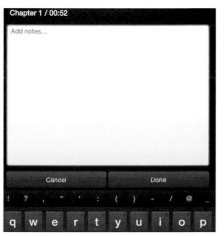

I The Note Editor. Tap Done to save the note.

Tap the Menu button to access the sleep timer **F**. With the sleep timer set, the audiobook will stop reading automatically after the selected duration or at the end of the current chapter **G**. Tap the Menu button and then Sleep Timer to change the time or to cancel the sleep timer.

5. You can leave this screen and use other functions of your Kindle Fire, and the audiobook will continue playing. Swipe down from the top of the Fire to bring up Quick Settings and the play controls for your audiobook.

To create a bookmark or note:

1. Start listening to an audiobook.

2. When you get to a moment in the audiobook that you want to bookmark, tap the Bookmark button to the right of the Play button **H**. An alert tells you that the bookmark has been inserted.

   If you want to take a note, long tap the Bookmark icon. Enter your note and tap Done **I**.

To edit notes and bookmarks:

1. Open an audiobook that contains bookmarks or notes.

2. Tap the Menu button and then tap View Bookmarks.

3. Both bookmarks and notes are listed . Tap a bookmark or note to start playing the audiobook at the point where it was inserted. Long tap either a note or a bookmark to see a menu . Tap Edit to add a note to your bookmark or edit the text of a note entered already. Tap Cancel to exit without saving the changes or Done to save your changes.

   Tap Delete to remove the bookmark or note.

To remove an audiobook:

1. Go to your Audiobooks library (Home screen > Audiobooks).

2. Long tap a downloaded audiobook. In the Cloud library, these are audiobooks with a check mark or any audiobook in the Device library .

3. Tap Remove from Device, and the audiobook is no longer stored on your Fire. You'll need to download it again to listen to it.

J All your bookmarks and notes are listed together.

K Long tap to edit or delete a bookmark.

L Long tap a downloaded audiobook and tap Remove from Device to delete it from the device.

Web

Accessing the Web with your Kindle Fire is easy: Tap Web, and Silk (the Web browser) launches. It allows you to search the Web and visit any page that you want.

Silk is unlike other browsers out there because it uses Amazon's cloud technology. Amazon gathers Silk usage data anonymously to make popular pages load faster and aggregate trending sites. These features let you stay on top of what's current. You can opt out of them so your usage isn't collected anonymously, or at all.

In this chapter

Using the Starter page

The *Starter page* is your jumping-off point for all browsing on the Fire. Whenever you open a new tab or load Silk without any content, the Starter page is displayed.

To use the Starter page:

1. Tap Web on the Home screen.

2. If you don't have any open tabs, the Starter page is displayed Ⓐ. There are three tabs at the top: Starter, Bookmarks, and History, with the active tab displayed in orange.

   The Starter tab is divided into three sections. The Most Visited section lists the sites that you visit most. If this is the first time you're using Silk, nothing will be listed. Trending Now represents sites that are being visited by lots of other Silk users. Selected Sites are sites that Amazon thinks people will find interesting.

   Each section displays thumbnails of the sites. Swipe left to see all the sites in each section. Tap a thumbnail to visit that site.

   Long tap a thumbnail to bring up a menu with a number of options Ⓑ. Tap Open to access the site in the current tab. "Open in new tab" creates an active tab and loads the site in it. The "Open in background tab" option will open a new tab behind the current tab and load the page. "Share link" opens the Sharing menu (more about this in the "Browsing" section). "Copy link URL" copies the site's address to your clipboard so you can paste it elsewhere. If you've visited this site before, a "Delete from history" action will be listed, which deletes the site from your browser history.

Ⓐ The Starter pages gives you a one-stop shop for your most visited pages, trending sites, and selected sites.

Ⓑ Long tap a thumbnail in the Starter page to access this menu.

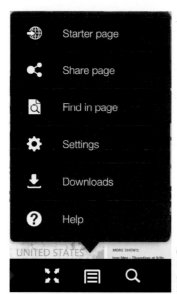

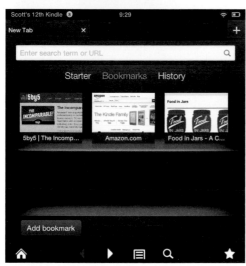

C Tap the Menu button to get back to the Starter page.

D Bookmarks in Grid View

TIP No matter where you are in the browser, tap the Menu button and then "Starter page" to return to the Starter page C.

To access bookmarks:

1. Open a Starter page.

2. Tap the Bookmarks tab D.

3. By default, all your bookmarks are displayed in a grid. To see them as a list, tap the Menu button and then List View E. You can also change the sort order by tapping the Menu button and then Sort Order. Tap the sort order you would like; by default, bookmarks are sorted by title, but if you would rather have the sites you visit most at the top, tap "Number of visits." If you want your recently used bookmarks handy, tap Last Accessed.

4. Tap a bookmark to load it.

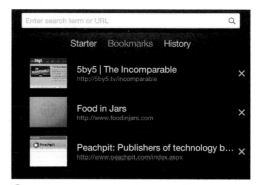

E Bookmarks in List View

To add a bookmark:

1. Open your bookmarks (Web > Starter Page > Bookmarks).
2. Tap "Add bookmark" .
3. Type in a name and the Web address **F**.
4. Tap OK, and your bookmark is saved.

To manage your bookmarks:

1. Open your bookmarks (Web > Starter Page > Bookmarks).
2. To delete or edit a bookmark in Grid View, long tap it **G**. Tap Delete. Tap Edit to change the name or Web address associated with the bookmark.

   If you want to delete more than one bookmark, switch to List View (Menu button > List View). Next to each bookmark is an x. Tap the x next to one of the bookmarks you want to delete **H**. The x turns orange, and two buttons appear at the bottom of the screen: "Clear selections" and "Delete marked items." Tap the x's next to the other bookmarks you want to delete and then tap "Delete marked items."

   The bookmarks are deleted immediately.

TIP To deselect a bookmark, tap the x.

F Add a bookmark by typing the name and URL. Tap OK to save.

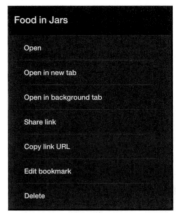

G Long tap a bookmark to see this menu.

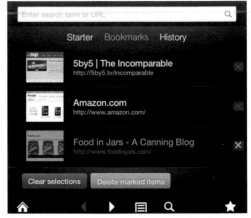

H Tap the box next to any number of bookmarks to select. Tap "Delete marked items" to delete them.

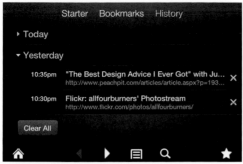

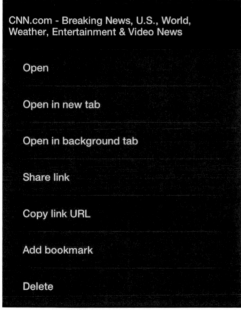

I Your browser history is grouped by date.

J Long tap a site in History to access this menu.

To manage your browsing history:

1. Open your bookmarks (Web > Starter Page > Bookmarks).

2. Tap History to see all the sites you've visited recently, grouped by date **I**.

   Tab the arrow next to a day to hide those sites. Tap again to list them.

3. Tap a site to visit it. Long tap to bring up the Site menu. You will see the option to delete the site from your history and remove it from your bookmarks (if the site is bookmarked) **J**.

   To clear all the sites from your history, tap the Clear All button on the lower-left corner. If you want to remove sites selectively, tap the x next to each relevant site. Tap the "Delete marked items" button that appears, and they are removed.

Browsing

Browsing the Web with Silk is more akin to browsing the Web from your computer rather than from a smartphone. The larger screen and processor power allow the Kindle Fire to give you a desktop experience on a mobile device. You don't have to stick with the mobile versions of websites with the Fire.

To use the URL bar:

1. Open Silk (Home screen > Web).

2. The URL bar is at the top of every page in Silk. Tap in it and start typing. As you type, Silk suggests searches, tries to predict what URL you're entering, and searches your history 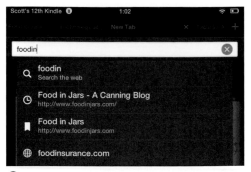. Each of the four different suggestions has icons to denote what they mean: Internet searches , URLs from your History , Bookmarks , and URL suggestions .

   Tap any of those to visit that site, or search for that term with the default search engine.

   Type the full URL and tap the Go button if none of the suggestions is appropriate.

3. The site loads in a tab. To reload a site, tap the Refresh button on the right side of the URL bar.

To bookmark a page:

1. With a site loaded in Silk, tap the Book-mark icon .

2. The title of the site is used for the name, and the URL is used for the location . Tap OK, and the bookmark is created.

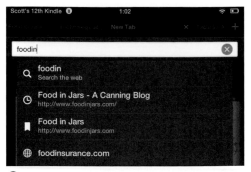

Ⓐ The URL bar allows you to search your history, the Internet, and bookmarks. You can also type a URL.

Ⓑ The Bookmark icon

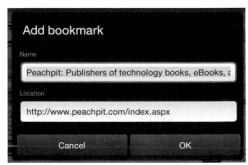

Ⓒ The name of the page is pulled from the title of the site when using this method to create a bookmark.

D The Full-screen icon

E A website is displayed in Full-screen mode.

To go full screen:

1. Open Silk (Home screen > Web).

2. Visit a site and tap the Full-screen button on the navigation bar **D**.

3. The URL and navigation bars are hidden, and all you see is the site **E**.

4. Tap the small handle at the bottom of the screen to exit Full-screen mode.

To zoom in on a site:

Place your thumb and index finger together on the screen and then move them apart. This will zoom in on the content. Pinch those fingers together to zoom out. You can also double tap a column of text or a picture to automatically zoom in on it.

To share a page:

1. Visit a page you want to share with someone in Silk (Home screen > Web).

2. Tap the Menu button and then "Share page."

3. Select the sharing method you would like to use from the Sharing menu . Keep in mind, the Sharing menu will list different options depending on which apps you have on your Kindle Fire.

4. A link to the page is pasted into whichever app you chose and is ready for sharing **G**.

To search within a Web page:

1. Open a website that you want to search (Home screen > Web).

2. Tap the Menu button and then "Find in page."

3. Type the word or phrase you're searching. All instances of the word or phrase are highlighted in yellow **H**. Tap the up and down arrows to cycle through the matches. The currently selected match is highlighted in orange.

4. Tap Done to close the page search.

F You can share a link easily using apps installed on your Kindle Fire that support this feature.

G An e-mail generated by the Share command

H Searching within a page

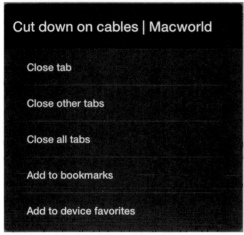

A The new Tab button

B The tab bar

Cut down on cables | Macworld

Close tab

Close other tabs

Close all tabs

Add to bookmarks

Add to device favorites

C Long tap a tab to see these options.

Working with tabs

Silk allows you to open multiple websites via *tabs*. One tab holds one website, but you can open up to ten tabs at any one time. You can switch between them to compare websites or open links behind the active tab to review later.

To create a new tab:

1. Open Silk (Home screen > Web).
2. Tap the + button in the upper-right corner **A**. A new tab opens with the Starter page loaded.

TIP To open a new tab from a link on a website, long tap the link and tap either "Open in new tab" or "Open in background tab."

To manage tabs:

1. Open Silk (Home screen > Web).
2. Silk remembers your open tabs automatically when you leave the app. If you have more than one tab open, they are arranged at the top of the screen **B**. Tap a tab to switch focus to it.

    Long tap a tab to get some more options **C**. Tap "Close tab" when you're done with it. "Close other tabs" will close all the tabs except the active one. "Add to bookmarks" and "Add to device favorites" will bookmark or add this site to your Favorites.

TIP As you open more and more tabs, the tab bar will fill up. Swipe to see all of your tabs.

3. When you're done with a tab, tap the x in the upper-right corner of the tab to close it.

To use Reading View:

1. Open Silk (Home screen > Web) and visit a website.

2. If the site you're on supports Reading View, a green icon will appear in the tab .

3. Tap the Reading View icon.

4. Silk grabs the text of the site, strips out all the website navigation and ads, and then displays just the text and inline images full screen **E**. Just like full-screen browsing, if you tap the small handle at the bottom of the screen, the navigation bar appears along with the tab bar. A new icon is on the navigation bar: Text settings **Aa**.

   Tap the Text settings icon, and some appearance options similar to those in Kindle books appear **F**.

5. When you're finished with Reading View, you may tap the Reading View icon in the tab if you aren't in Full-screen mode. Instead, you may tap the x in the upper-right corner. You're returned to the normal Silk view of the page.

TIP Reading View works best on articles from newspapers, magazines, and blogs.

D The Reading View icon appears on a page that is supported.

Compact cable kits

Short cables are lightweight, take up less space in a bag, and are less likely to tangle. Thankfully, it's no longer necessary to hunt down short versions of essential cables on your own, as a number of companies sell handy kits.

Micro, mini, 30: I previously covered Griffin Technology's $25 USB Mini Cable Kit, Incase's USB Mini Cable Kit which offers three short (3.5-inch) USB cables in one package. Incase's $25 USB Mini Cable Kit contains 4-inch versions—the length includes the connectors—of the same three cables: USB-to-30-pin (dock connector) for iPads and pre-2012 iPhones and iPods; USB-to-Micro-USB; and USB-to-Mini-USB. The actual cable sections are thinner than those of Griffin's, making Incase's cables

E An article in Reading View

F You can change these appearance settings when using Reading View.

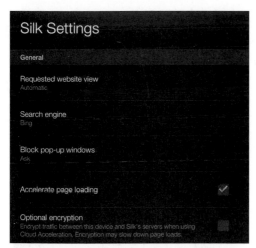

A The General settings cover basic functionality.

B Saved Data settings control what is saved.

Customizing settings

Silk has a large number of settings that impact its functionality. You can turn off the functionality that talks to Amazon's servers (this will speed up your browsing), clear your cookies and caches, and turn off images and security warnings.

To modify the cloud features of Silk:

1. Open Silk (Home screen > Web).
2. Tap the Menu button and then Settings.
3. The General settings section groups settings that impact the overall use of Silk A.
4. Uncheck the "Accelerate page loading" box to have your Web requests sent to websites directly instead of using Amazon's servers. (Amazon's servers do some technical wizardry to speed up browsing.)

To clear your saved data:

1. Launch Silk (Home screen > Web).
2. Tap the Menu button and then Settings.
3. As you browse, cookies are set. Silk caches data to speed your browsing and remembers passwords for you. The Saved Data settings control what Silk remembers for you B. Tap "Clear history," Cache, Passwords, or "Clear all cookie data" to erase that data from Silk. A confirmation appears to make sure you really want to clear this data.

TIP You can also disable location access here by unchecking "Enable location."

To request full versions of sites all the time:

1. By default, Silk identifies itself to a site and allows the site to determine whether Silk will load the mobile or desktop version. Launch Silk (Home screen > Web).

2. Tap the Menu button and then Settings.

3. Tap Requested Website View in General Settings 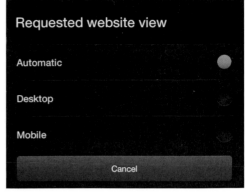.

4. Tap Desktop to request the full version of a site **C**.

C You can tell Silk to automatically select the type of website to display. You can also choose Desktop or Mobile manually.

13

Photos

The Photos library on the Kindle Fire gathers pictures from a variety of places, such as your Amazon Cloud Drive, Facebook, downloaded images from the Internet, saved attachments, and screenshots.

You can view, delete, and share photos on your Fire, but the device doesn't offer any native photo-editing abilities. Search the Amazon Appstore for photo-editing apps if you need one.

In this chapter

Importing photos

When you first get your Kindle Fire and tap Photos on the Home screen, you'll see a stock image that Amazon includes. You need to add photos to your Cloud or Device library.

> **TIP** The Kindle Fire supports three image formats: JPEG, PNG, and GIF.

To use Cloud Drive to import your photos:

1. Go to http://amazon.com/clouddrive on your Mac or PC.

2. Log into your Cloud Drive with your Amazon account **B**.

Cloud Drive

Included with your Amazon account, for no additional charge, is 5GB of space on Amazon's Cloud Drive (servers), where you can upload any manner of files **A**. Amazon has native Cloud Drive clients for Windows and OS X as well as a Web client.

You can use this space to store anything you would like, and it will become available automatically on your Kindle Fire. Amazon offers additional space for a yearly fee. Visit http://amazon.com/clouddrive for more information.

A The Amazon Cloud Drive logo

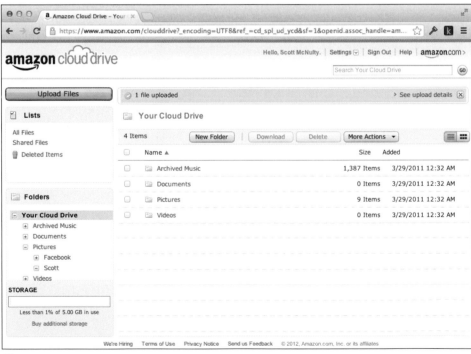

B Cloud Drive on the Web

C Uploading a file to Cloud Drive

3. Click the Pictures folder. Any photos uploaded to this folder will appear in your Kindle Fire's Photos Cloud library.

4. You can upload photos to this folder directly or create a new folder by clicking the Create New Folder button. All folders in the Pictures folder become albums on your Kindle Fire.

   Click the Upload File button. The folder you're currently viewing is selected as the destination. Click the menu to select another folder **C**. Click "Select files" to upload. Find the files you'd like to upload in your computer's file system and click Upload to perform that action.

TIP Files larger than 2GB cannot be uploaded to your Cloud Drive.

5. On your Kindle Fire, open the Photos Library (Home screen > Photos). The photo(s) you uploaded will be in the Pictures album in the Cloud library.

To import Facebook photos:

1. Link your Facebook account to your Kindle Fire (see Chapter 1 for details on how to do this).

2. Open your Photos Cloud library (Home screen > Photos > Cloud).

3. Tap the Menu button and then Import .

4. Importing your Facebook photos, including your albums, can take some time depending on how many photos you have **E**. Tap OK to import.

5. Your Facebook photos and albums appear in your Cloud library in an album titled Facebook. They are also imported into your Cloud Drive.

TIP Importing Facebook photos and albums is a manual process. When you upload new photos to Facebook, they aren't imported into your Fire Photos library automatically. You'll need to repeat this process, though only new pictures are imported.

D Tap the Import button to get your Facebook photos onto your Kindle Fire.

E Depending on your wireless connection and number of Facebook photos, this process could take some time.

To download photos from your Cloud library:

1. Find a photo using Silk or in your Cloud library on your Kindle Fire.

2. Long tap a photo or an album.

3. Tap Download **F**.

4. The photo or album is downloaded and listed in your Device library.

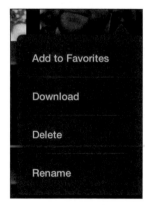

F Long tap and then tap Download to save the pictures to your Fire.

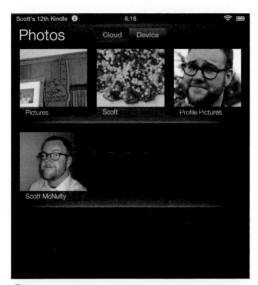

A Albums in the Cloud Photos library

B Inside an album the pictures are shown, as well as the name of the album.

C Tapping a picture displays it. Tap the album name to return to the album list.

Viewing photos

Now that you have some photos on your Fire, you need to know how to view them. There are two libraries: Cloud and Device. The Cloud library shows all your photos from your Cloud Drive, stored on Amazon. The photos in your Device library are stored on your Fire's memory.

All your photos are organized into albums that are either created by the Fire or reflect those you created on Facebook. Tap the album to see all the photos that it contains.

To view or zoom your photos:

1. Open a Photos library (Home screen > Photos).

2. All your albums are listed **A**. Tap the Menu button and then Sort by Date to change the sorting. Tap About to sort by album name.

3. Tap an album to see all the photos listed **B**. Notice at the top, the album you're in currently is shown. Tap Photos to go back to your main library.

4. Tap a photo to view it **C**. Pinch to zoom in and out to examine the photos.

   At the top of the photo, you'll see the name of the album that contains the photo and how many pictures are in the album.

   Swipe left or right to look at the other photos in the album.

5. Tap the Back button to return to your Photos library.

To switch between Grid and Mosaic Views:

1. Open your Photos library (Home screen > Photos).

2. Tap an album.

3. When you hold your Fire in portrait mode, the photos are displayed in a grid. Hold the Fire in landscape, and the photos are displayed in a mosaic . Swipe to see all the pictures in the mosaic. Tap a photo to see it full screen.

D Photos in an album are displayed in a mosaic when your Fire is in landscape mode.

To rename albums:

1. Open your Photos library (Home screen > Photos).

2. Long tap an album.

3. Tap Rename.

4. Type in a new name for the folder and tap Rename **E**. The album now has a new name.

E Albums can be renamed. Type a new name and tap Rename.

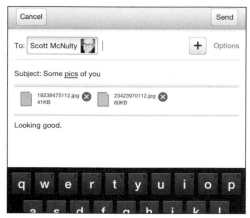

 The E-mail icon in the navigation bar

B Tap to select the photos you'd like to e-mail.

C An e-mail with the selected photos attached

Managing photos

You've imported, saved, and viewed photos. Now, all that remains is sharing them with your friends and deleting photos you don't want anymore.

To e-mail photos:

1. Open your Photos library (Home screen > Photos).

2. Tap an album to see all the photos it holds.

3. Tap the E-mail icon in the navigation bar **A**.

4. Tap the photos you want to e-mail. A check mark appears on the selected photos **B**.

TIP Tap a selected photo to unselect it.

5. Tap the "Send photos" button.

6. Type the e-mail address, a subject, and a body into the e-mail message with the files attached **C**.

7. Tap Send.

To delete photos:

1. Open your Photos library (Home screen > Photos).

2. Tap an album to see all the photos it holds.

3. Tap the Delete icon .

4. Tap all the photos you want to delete to select them.

5. Tap Delete Photos, and the photos are deleted.

D The Delete icon in the navigation bar

Docs

The *Docs library*, short for personal documents library, holds documents from places other than Amazon. The e-books you purchase from publishers' sites directly and your Word documents are all stored in the Docs library.

There are a few ways to get documents into Docs: by e-mail, via your Cloud Drive, or by transferring the files via USB.

In this chapter

E-mailing documents

E-mail is one of the easiest ways to get personal documents on your Kindle Fire. Every Kindle (both Fire and non-Fire models) are assigned a unique e-mail address. Send an e-mail to that address with an attachment, and after a few moments, the attached document appears in your Docs Cloud library.

A Your Kindle Fire's e-mail address is displayed at the top of the Docs library.

To find your Kindle Fire's e-mail address:

1. Go to your Docs library (Home screen > Docs).

2. Your Kindle Fire's e-mail address is listed at the top of the Docs Cloud library **A**.

To e-mail files to your Kindle Fire:

1. Compose an e-mail to your Kindle Fire's e-mail address.

2. Attach a document; Microsoft Word, HTML, RTF, MOBI, and PDF are common file types. If you want to send more than one file to your Fire, you can compress (ZIP) the files that you attach to the e-mail.

3. Send the e-mail. No subject or body is needed.

4. Amazon will convert Word, HTML, and RTF files to Kindle format for delivery to your Kindle Fire. PDFs and MOBI files are sent to the Fire's Cloud library in their original formats.

Your Kindle Account

Manage Your Devices
Subscription Settings
Kindle Payment Settings
Personal Document Settings
Country Settings

B Your Kindle Account on Amazon.com

Approved Personal Document E-mail List
To prevent spam, your Kindle will only receive files from the following e-mail addresses you have authorized. Learn more
E-mail address   Actions
                                                                  Delete
                                                                  Delete
                                                                  Delete
                                                                  Delete
                                                                  Delete
Add a new approved e-mail address

C The Approved Personal Document E-mail List determines who can e-mail documents to your Kindle Fire.

Add a new approved e-mail address

Enter an approved e-mail address.
Tip: Enter a partial address, such as @yourcompany.com, to authorize multiple senders.

E-mail address:

Add Address

June 23, 2009

D Enter an e-mail address and click Add Address.

Send-to-Kindle E-Mail Settings
You can e-mail personal documents to the following Kindle(s) using the e-mail addresses shown. Learn more
Name ▼   E-mail Address   Actions
Scott McNulty's iPad 3   smcnulty_63@kindle.com   Edit
Scott McNulty's iPhone 2   smcnulty_13@kindle.com   Edit
Scott's 10th Kindle   smcnulty_90@kindle.com   Edit

E Send-to-Kindle E-Mail Settings lists all of your Kindle's e-mail addresses.

Edit Send-to-Kindle E-mail Address

Edit the Send-to-Kindle e-mail address used to send personal documents to this Kindle.

Send-to-Kindle E-mail Address: smcnulty_387   @kindle.com

Update   Cancel

F You can make your Send-to-Kindle address whatever you like, as long as it isn't already in use by another Kindle user.

To limit which addresses can send docs to your Kindle Fire:

1. If you would like to limit which e-mail addresses can send files to your Fire, log into the Manage Your Kindle website with your Amazon account (www.amazon.com/manageyourkindle).

2. Click Personal Document Settings in the Your Kindle Account **B**.

3. Scroll down to the Approved Personal Document E-mail list **C**. Only e-mails on this list are allowed to send documents to your Kindles.

TIP This list applies to all your Kindles.

4. Click "Add a new approved e-mail address."

5. Enter the e-mail address you want to add and click Add Address **D**. If you want to allow e-mail from an entire domain (say, from all of Disney), add @disney.com to your Approved Personal Document E-mail list.

To change your Kindle Fire's e-mail address:

1. If you don't like the e-mail address assigned to your Kindle Fire, just change it. Log into the Manage Your Kindle website.

2. Click Personal Document Settings.

3. Scroll to Send-to-Kindle Settings **E**.

4. All of your Kindles and their e-mail addresses are listed. Click the Edit link next to the e-mail address you'd like to change.

5. Enter a new address and click Update **F**.

Sending documents via Cloud Drive

Anyone with an Amazon account gets 5GB of space on Amazon's cloud. Amazon calls this space *Cloud Drive* and allows you to upload any kind of files you like. All documents uploaded to your Cloud Drive are added to your Docs Cloud library automatically. All you have to do is upload it; Amazon takes care of the rest.

To add documents using Cloud Drive:

1. Log into your Cloud Drive from your computer (www.amazon.com/clouddrive).

   TIP You can also install the Mac or PC Cloud Drive app.

2. Click Upload Files, and choose the files you want to upload .

3. Click Open, and the files are uploaded.

4. Wait a few moments, and the document appears in the Cloud library of your Kindle Fire.

   TIP If you create a folder in your Cloud Drive and upload the documents to it, that folder will appear in your Cloud library when you tap By Folder **B**. All the files inside will be listed.

A Clicking the Upload Files button adds files to your Cloud Drive.

B When you create folders on your Cloud Drive, they are reflected in your Docs library.

Sideloading documents

Sending documents to your Kindle Fire via e-mail or the Send to Kindle app requires your Kindle to have an active Internet connection. If you want to transfer documents to your Kindle Fire directly, you can always sideload them.

To sideload documents:

1. Plug a micro-USB cable into your Kindle Fire, and plug the USB side into a USB port on your computer.

2. The Fire will show up as a device in Windows; on your Mac, the Android File Transfer app will appear (see Chapter 7 for more details).

3. Click the Documents folder on the Kindle Fire.

4. Drag and drop all the documents you want to transfer into the Documents folder on your Kindle Fire.

5. The documents are now available in the Docs Device library.

TIP **Documents transferred to your Kindle using this method aren't saved to the cloud, so they won't be available to your other Kindles.**

Reading and deleting documents

Reading documents on your Kindle Fire is very much like reading books. The Docs library has two parts: Cloud and Device. Documents from the Cloud library must be downloaded before you can read them (downloaded docs have a check mark next to them). Either library can be sorted by the same four criteria: name, recent, type (PDF, DOC, or Kindle, for example), and folder.

Every doc in the library displays its file type, title, author, how far into it you've read, and whether or not it has been downloaded to the device.

Long tap a doc to find out whether it is in your Cloud Drive or your Kindle Archive .

Ⓐ Long tapping a document will tell you if it is on your Cloud Drive or in your Kindle Archive.

B Word documents open in OfficeSuite

To read a document:

- When you tap a Kindle or PDF document, it opens in the Reading app on your Fire. Turning the page works just like it does in a book: tap the right or left side of the screen to page forward or back.

  Kindle files allow you to change all the same settings as Kindle books and add notes, highlights, and bookmarks (see Chapter 7).

  PDFs are faithful representations of the print version, so you can't change anything about their appearance. You can't select text or add notes, highlights, or bookmarks either.

- Word docs are opened in the OfficeSuite app, which is included with your Fire **B**. This app lets you read Word documents but not edit them. You can zoom in by pinching, and you can scroll through the pages by swiping up and down.

> **TIP** If you want to edit Word documents, you can purchase OfficeSuite Pro from the Amazon Appstore.

To delete documents:

- Documents stored in your Cloud Drive will be deleted from your Kindle Fire if you delete them from your Cloud Drive.

- Docs in your Kindle Archive are listed in your Kindle library on the Manage Your Kindle website. Log into that website to delete personal documents. (See Chapter 7 for detailed instructions.)

- Long tap a downloaded document on your Kindle Fire to find the Remove from Device option .

C Tap Remove from Device to delete the document from your Kindle.

15

Offers

Amazon is able to sell the Kindle Fire at the price point it does, in part, because of *offers*. Offers are advertisements that appear on the Lock screen of your Kindle Fire for a variety of services. These offers are updated over time, so you'll see a variety of goods and services advertised on your Kindle Fire's Lock screen.

Some might wonder why Amazon calls them "offers" instead of advertisements. In addition to displaying traditional ads, Amazon uses the offers functionality to give Kindle Fire owners access to special deals. For example, owners might receive $5 credits for music, discounts on Kindle books, and the like.

In this chapter

Redeeming offers

Whether your Kindle Fire is displaying an ad or an offer on your Lock screen, all the offers provide a way to get more information about the offer or product they are advertising.

You can also see all the current offers on your Kindle Fire, and find out more information about them, by tapping the Offers library.

To open an offer on the Lock screen:

1. Make sure your Kindle Fire is locked.

2. On the right is the Unlock swipe, and on the left is the swipe to find out more about the offer **A**.

3. Swipe to the left, and you'll be taken to a page where you can redeem an offer, find out more about the advertised product, or even watch a movie trailer.

To see all offers currently available on your Fire:

1. Unlock your device and tap Offers.

2. All your current offers are displayed **B**.

3. Tap an offer to see more information.

TIP You must have an active Internet connection to access details about offers.

A An offer is displayed on the Lock screen.

B The Offers library lists what's available.

A Your Kindle Account on the Manage Your Kindle website

B The list of your registered Kindles is associated with your Amazon account.

Unsubscribe from Special Offers & Sponsored Screensavers

This Kindle is currently subscribed to Special Offers and was purchased at a subsidized price ($15 discount).

Amazon is able to offer the Kindle at a subsidized price by delivering Special Offers & Sponsored Screensavers.

By unsubscribing you will be charged $15 (plus applicable tax).

Unsubscribe now with 1-Click®   Cancel

C Unsubscribing from the Offers program on your Kindle Fire will cost you a small fee.

Opting out of offers

Many people find the offers on their Kindle Fires to be useful, or at least inoffensive. However, if you want an offer-free Fire experience, you can opt out of the program. Because the Offers program subsidizes the price, there is a charge associated with turning off offers on your Kindle Fire.

To turn off offers:

1. Log into the Manage Your Kindle website with your Amazon account (www.amazon/manageyourkindle).

2. Click Manage Your Devices under Your Kindle Account **A**.

3. This page lists all your registered Kindles and some more information **B**. There is a column called Special Offers. Find your Kindle Fire, and notice that it says Subscribed in the Special Offers column.

4. Click Edit next to Subscribed.

5. The Unsubscribe box appears and lets you know how much it will cost to turn off the offers' screensavers (in this case, $15) **C**. Click the Unsubscribe now with 1-Click button.

6. A green alert lets you know your Fire has been unsubscribed **D**.

continues on next page

Unsubscribed Scott's 12th Kindle from Special Offers. After payment is confirmed, connect Kindle to Wi-Fi to complete the process.

D When you unsubscribe, complete the process by connecting your Fire to a network.

7. Unlock your Fire and connect to a Wi-Fi network.

8. After a moment, a notification appears letting you know that your Fire has been unsubscribed from Offers .

9. The Offers library disappears from the navigation bar, and your Lock screen now displays a variety of high-quality images instead of offers **F**.

E A notification appears on your Kindle Fire when you've unsubscribed from the Offers program. You can no longer access the Offers library.

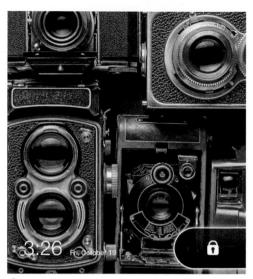

F The Lock screen now displays a selection of high-resolution pictures.

16

Communication

The Kindle Fire is not only great at consuming media but is also useful for keeping in touch with the people in your life. The built-in E-mail, Calendar, and Contacts apps support a wide variety of e-mail services. With these apps, you can check your e-mail, sync your contacts, and access your calendar.

In this chapter

Using accounts

You need to set up some accounts before you can access e-mail, contacts, or the calendar on your Kindle Fire. The Fire currently supports the following accounts and associated functionality:

- **AOL:** This supports e-mail only.

- **Exchange:** Generally used by companies, Exchange support on the Fire includes e-mail, contacts, and a calendar.

- **Gmail:** Google's e-mail offering fully supports e-mail, contacts, and a calendar.

- **Hotmail:** Now known as Outlook.com, this service from Microsoft includes e-mail, contact, and calendar support on the Fire.

- **Yahoo!:** Only e-mail and contacts are supported for an account associated with this venerable Web portal.

- **Other:** If your ISP or employer (who doesn't use Exchange) offers you an e-mail account, this is the option for you. Only e-mail is supported.

To add an account:

1. Swipe down to bring up Quick Settings, and tap More.

2. Tap My Account.

3. Tap Manage E-mail Accounts 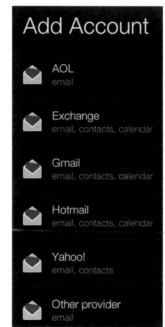.

4. Tap Add Account.

5. Select your mail provider from the list of options **B**. If you tap "Other provider," see the "Other e-mail accounts" sidebar for more information.

A The My Account settings is a one-stop shop for all things account related.

B You can add various accounts to your Kindle.

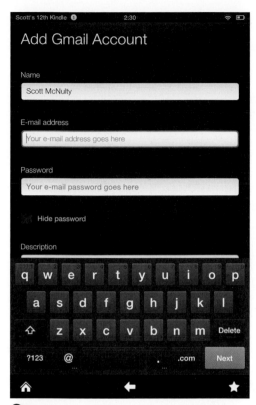

C When you add an account, you need to tell your Fire some information about it.

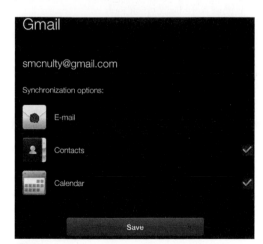

D Some account types sync more than just e-mail; however, you can pick and choose.

6. Enter your name (this is auto filled, but you can change it if you like), e-mail address, password, and description of the account. Tap Next **C**.

7. Choose which services in addition to e-mail that you want to synchronize with your Kindle. Tap Save **D**.

continues on next page

8. Setup is complete **E**. Tap View Inbox to hop right into your e-mail, or tap "Go to account settings" to make changes to the setup. Tap "Add another account" if you would like to perform that action.

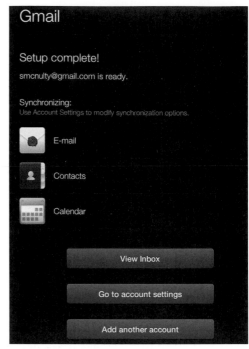

E Setup is complete. Tap View Inbox to jump right into your e-mail.

Other e-mail accounts

If your e-mail provider isn't listed in the account creation section, chances are you can still check your e-mail on your Kindle Fire. You'll have to enter your e-mail account settings manually using either POP3 or IMAP. Both methods require you to know a bit more about the server settings needed to check your e-mail.

Check with your e-mail provider to see what the correct settings are for your e-mail account.

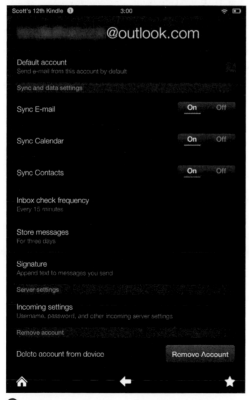

F All the accounts currently set up on your Kindle Fire are listed under the Add Account button.

G Settings for an Outlook.com account include the same options as other account types.

To change account settings:

1. Swipe down to access Quick Settings, and tap More.

2. Tap My Account.

3. Tap Manage E-mail Accounts **A**.

4. All the accounts on your Kindle Fire are listed under the Add Account button **F**. Tap the account you want to modify.

5. The settings allow you to change a number of things about how this account works **G**.

   The first section of settings controls which name appears on the e-mails you send, the description of the account on your Fire, and whether this account is the default. Tap Your Name or Description to change either one. Tap the box next to Default Account to send e-mails from this account by default.

   The "Sync and data settings" section allows you to control what is being synced with this account and how often. Tap Off next to E-mail, Calendar, or Contacts to stop syncing them with your Kindle.

continues on next page

Tap "Inbox check frequency" to set how often your e-mail is checked 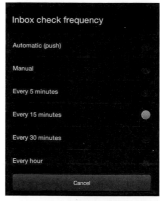. Automatic will deliver e-mail to your Fire as it arrives; Manual checks only when you initiate an e-mail check; and the others check on a schedule.

Tap "Store messages" to set how much of your e-mail the Fire will store and make available for you.

Tap Signature to have some text appended automatically to e-mails sent from this account. Each account may have different signatures. You may have one for work and another for your personal account .

Finally, you can tap "Server settings" to change your e-mail server settings manually.

To delete an account:

1. Swipe down to access Quick Settings, and tap More.

2. Tap My Account.

3. Tap Manage E-mail Accounts **A**.

4. All the accounts on your Kindle Fire are listed under the Add Account button **E**. Tap the account you want to delete.

5. Go to the bottom of the settings and tap the Remove Account button **J**.

6. Everything associated with the account will be removed, so a confirmation is displayed **K**. Tap OK to remove or Cancel to keep the account.

H How often do you want your Fire to check your e-mail?

I You can set per-account e-mail signatures.

J Removing an account is as simple as tapping Remove Account.

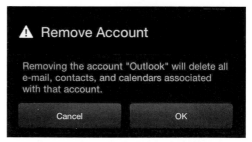

K All data related to that account is removed as well, so be sure you want to remove it.

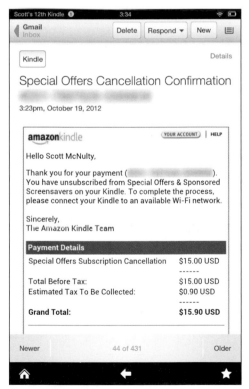

A The E-mail icon included with the Kindle Fire

B A Gmail Inbox with unread e-mails shown in bold

C Reading an HTML e-mail

E-mailing

E-mail works on your Kindle Fire much like it does on other systems that you use. All e-mail sent from the Fire's built-in E-mail program is sent in plain text; no fancy formatting is supported. However, you can still read HTML e-mails (such as newsletters and the like) on the Fire without any difficulty.

To read an e-mail:

1. Tap Apps on the Home screen.

2. Tap the E-mail app icon **A**.

3. If you have an e-mail account set up, you'll be taken to the default account's Inbox **B**.

   Your messages are displayed in a list, with the newest messages at the top and unread messages bolded. The sender, subject, and first few characters of the e-mail are shown. Swipe to scroll, and tap an e-mail to read it **C**.

continues on next page

At the bottom of the e-mail is a Newer button, the position of this e-mail relative to the rest in your Inbox, and an Older button. Tap either the Newer or Older button to load the e-mail you received right after or before this one.

At the top of the screen are a Delete button, the Respond button, a New button, and the Settings button. Tap the Delete button to get rid of this e-mail, the Respond button to reply to or forward the e-mail, and the New button to start an e-mail.

Tap Details to see more information about the recipient of the e-mail **D**. Tap the sender or receiver to see their e-mail address and add them to your contacts **E**.

TIP If the e-mail has an attachment, tap its file name to download it; long tap for some options **F**.

4. Tap the Inbox button at the top left to return to your Inbox.

D The sender and receiver details

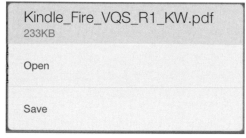

E Tap the sender of an e-mail to add them to your contacts.

F Long tap an attachment's file name to open it or save it.

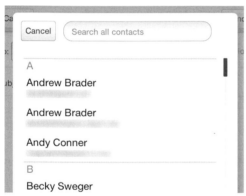

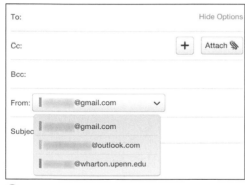

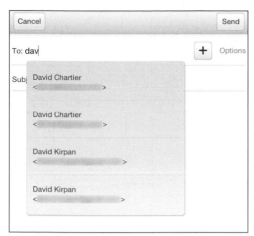

G As you type, e-mail addresses or names of suggested contacts appear.

H You can search your contacts for e-mail addresses to add to your e-mail.

I Select a From account for this e-mail.

To send an e-mail:

1. Launch the E-mail app.

2. You're taken to your default e-mail account. Tap the New button.

3. A blank message opens. Tap the To field and start typing the e-mail address or name of this e-mail's recipient **G**. As you type, your contacts are being searched and suggestions appear. Tap a suggested contact to add them to this e-mail, or just finish typing the e-mail address.

   Tap + to search your contacts directly **H**.

   Tap Show Options to see the Cc and Bcc fields. Tap in either and type in addresses to Cc or Bcc people.

   Tap the From drop-down to change the e-mail account from which this e-mail will be sent. This appears only if you have more than one account set up **I**.

4. Type a subject and your message.

5. Tap Send when your message is complete, and off it goes. You're returned to the Inbox.

To send an attachment:

1. Create a new e-mail, and add recipients, a subject, and message if desired.

2. Tap Options.

3. Tap the Attach button .

4. Choose the app that contains the file you want to attach ⓙ. This list varies depending on the apps you have installed on your Kindle. In this case, we'll tap Photos.

5. Tap the file you want to e-mail from the app, and it is attached to the e-mail message.

6. Repeat as necessary.

TIP Tap the x next to the attachment to remove it from the e-mail ⓚ.

7. Tap Send when you're finished.

To search your e-mail:

1. Open the Inbox you want to search.

2. Tap the Search icon at the bottom of the screen.

3. Tap Subject, From, or To and type what you are searching ⓛ.

4. Tap the e-mail you want to open.

TIP You can switch from searching Subjects to the From/To fields by tapping them. The search results update.

ⓙ Attach files by selecting them from the listed apps.

ⓚ You can remove an attachment from an e-mail by tapping the x.

ⓛ Search your e-mail by the Subject, From, or To field.

M Mark e-mails as read or unread and star them.

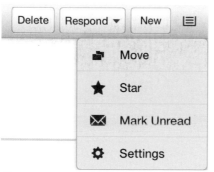

N All folders in your e-mail account show up in this list.

O The menu on an individual e-mail message

To manage your Inbox:

1. Each e-mail has a box to its left. Tap a box to select an e-mail.

2. With at least one e-mail selected, three buttons appear at the top of the e-mail list: Delete, Move, and Mark **M**.

   Tap Delete to get rid of the selected messages.

   Tap Move to relocate the selected messages to a different folder in the account **N**. You cannot create new folders here; just move messages to existing folders.

   Tap Mark to mark the messages as read or unread. You may also add or remove stars from them **M**.

TIP You may move and star individual messages. Tap them, and then tap the Settings button on the top right to see your options **O**.

To switch e-mail accounts or folders:

- In portrait orientation, tap the button at the top left of the screen. The account or folder you're looking at will display (the Inbox, at the moment). The account or folder list is revealed 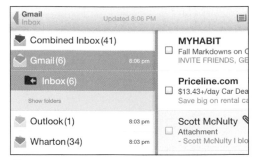. Tap Show folders to see the complete list of folders. Tap a folder to see its contents. Tap the button in the top left to return to the previous folder.

- When viewing e-mail in landscape mode, the folder or account list is displayed by default. Tapping the top-left button hides the account or folder list and displays your e-mail list with the message content displayed to the right 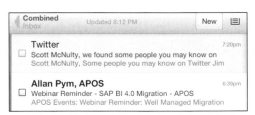.

P The accounts and folders list

To see all new e-mails across accounts:

1. Launch the E-mail app.
2. Go to the accounts list (see previous task).
3. Tap Combined Inbox **R**. All e-mails from the Inboxes of your various accounts are displayed. A color band appears next to each message indicating the target account.

Q The Inbox in landscape mode lists messages on the left and previews their contents on the right.

To change e-mail settings:

1. Open the Inbox of the e-mail account whose settings you would like to change.
2. Tap the Menu button at the top right of the screen **O**.
3. Tap Settings.
4. Tap E-mail General Settings **S**.

   Tap one of the text sizes to change the default. You can also toggle on or off showing embedded images, downloading attachments, and including original messages in replies.

R The Combined Inbox lists e-mails from all your accounts.

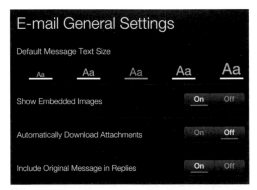

S E-mail General Settings apply to all of your accounts.

A The Calendar icon displays the current date and day.

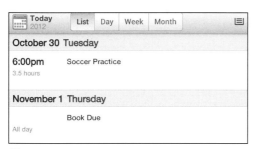

B The four different calendar views are always listed at the top of the screen.

C List View displays all your events.

D Day, Week, and Month all include a navigation area at the bottom so you can jump to different dates easily.

Calendaring

The Calendar app displays all your appointments in a list, daily, weekly, or monthly view. When you edit or add items to a calendar on your Fire, those changes will be reflected wherever else you can view that synced calendar. (In other words, if it is a Google calendar, your changes will show up on the Web version.)

To view your calendar and events:

1. Go to the Apps library and launch the Calendar app **A**.

TIP The Calendar icon displays the current date and day.

2. Along the top of the calendar, you'll find four buttons: List, Day, Week, and Month **B**. Tap a view, and the calendar changes. Tapping Today always takes you back to the current day on your calendar.

3. In List View, you swipe to see all the events in the future or the past **C**. The other three views support swiping as well, but they also have a date navigation at the bottom (portrait) or side (landscape) where you can tap a date and just jump to it **D**.

4. All of your calendar events are listed. If you have more than one calendar account on your Fire, the events are color coded with a stripe so you know which events correspond to a particular calendar.

continues on next page

5. Tap an event to see more details **E**.

6. Tap the top-left button to return to your Calendar View.

TIP When you're viewing an event, tap **Respond > Reply all** to send an e-mail to everyone invited.

To add an event:

1. Open your calendar.

2. Tap the Menu button in the upper-right corner **F**.

TIP By default, the calendar shows all the events from all your calendar accounts with colored stripes to differentiate them. Tap the Settings menu and then **Calendars to Display** to pick which ones you want to see.

3. Tap New Event.

4. Fill in the title of your event and then set a start and end time **G**. Tap the "All day" box if this is a full-day event. You can set up repeating events by tapping the Repeat menu and selecting a time period to repeat this event **H**.

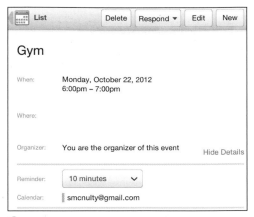

E The details of an event

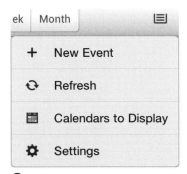

F Menu options

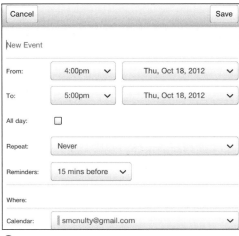

G The New Event form

H Time periods available for repeating events

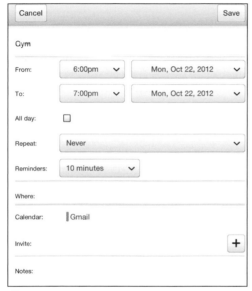

I Event reminders appear in the Notifications section.

J Editing an event

K Tap an event to delete or edit it.

Set a reminder by tapping the menu and selecting from it. Type the location and select the calendar where you want to save this event (the default account's calendar is selected automatically).

If you need to invite people to a meeting, type their e-mail address (or names if they are in your contacts), or tap + to search your contacts directly.

Finally, typing a note can be useful when you're scheduling a meeting with others. Tap Save.

To use reminders:

1. When an event has a reminder, it appears in the notifications at the appointed time **I**.

2. Tap the notification to go to the full-event entry.

To edit an event:

1. Open your calendar and find the event you want to edit.

2. Tap the event and then tap Edit. Here, you can change any of the event settings **J**.

3. Tap Save, and all your changes are preserved. Any invitees are updated.

To delete an event:

1. Open your calendar and find the event you want to delete.

2. Tap the event **K**.

3. Tap the Delete button on the event details. The event is removed from your calendar.

To change calendar settings:

1. Launch the Calendar app.

2. Tap the Menu button and then Settings.

3. Tap Calendar General Settings 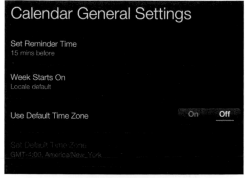.

4. Here, you can set the default reminder time; indicate the day on which the week starts (Locale default, Saturday, Sunday, or Monday); disable the default time zone and set a custom one for the calendar **M**.

L Calendar General Settings

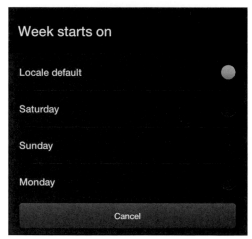

M Set your week-start day.

Using the Contacts app

The Contacts app lists information, such as address and phone number, for the different people in your life. Most account types can sync contacts, so you can enter changes on your Fire and they show up on any device linked to that account. You can also choose to have your contact data on the Fire only.

To set up your profile:

1. Launch the Contacts app from the Apps library **A**.

2. If you don't have a profile set up, you'll see "Set up my profile" at the top of the Contacts list **B**. Tap it.

3. The profile tells your Kindle Fire about you. Fill out this form with your information including first and last name, address, and contact information. Tap the down arrow next to "First name" to enter more detailed information **C**.

   Tap "Add organization" to include your company name and title. Tap the placeholder icon in the upper-right corner to add a photo to your profile **D**. Tap Photos to choose from your Photos library on the Fire. If you've added your Facebook photos, you should have a number of good options.

continues on next page

A The Contacts icon

B Your profile tells the Fire who you are.

C Your local profile has the same fields as any other contact on your Fire.

D Use one of the listed apps to select a photo for your profile.

4. Swipe down and tap Add Another Field to include a variety of additional fields including Phonetic name, Nickname, and IM (instant messaging). These options are available for all contacts, not just your profile.

5. Tap Save, and your profile is created .

E When your profile is filled in, your name and picture will appear at the top of your contacts.

To search contacts:

1. Launch the Contacts app.

2. Swipe down to see your contacts listed in alphabetical order. You can scroll through them like this and tap a contact to see more information. Tap the Search icon in the navigation bar to search.

3. As you type your query, the contacts are filtered **F**. Tap the contact you want to see. Tap the x to clear your search and see all your contacts.

TIP Tap "Search contacts on server" to continue your search in any server-based address books that might be associated with your account.

To browse contacts:

1. Launch the Contacts app.

2. Swipe up and down to scroll through the list of contacts. Tap and drag on the scroll bar to scroll quickly through the list **G**. As you scroll through alphabetical sections, the letter of the group you're in currently hovers on the side.

   By default, contacts are sorted by first name; to change this, adjust the settings (see "To change contact settings").

3. Tap the contact whose details you want to see.

F As you type to search, your contacts are filtered.

G Scroll through your contacts quickly by tapping and dragging the scroll bar.

H These buttons are available when you tap a contact.

I Editing a contact allows you to add and remove information.

J When you create a contact on your Kindle, the device needs to sync to one of your accounts.

K You can add contacts to any of your accounts.

To edit a contact:

1. Launch the Contacts app.

2. Find the contact you want to edit and tap it.

3. Tap the Edit button **H**.

4. All the fields in the contact, including the picture, are now editable **I**. Swipe down to the "Add additional" fields to include more information. Tap the x next to a field to remove it.

5. Tap Save when you're finished editing, and the contact has been updated.

To create a contact:

1. Launch the Contacts app.

2. Tap the New button at the top of the contacts list.

3. Contacts sync to an account; choose an account here **J**. This list mirrors the e-mail accounts you have set up on your Fire. If you don't have any accounts set up, you can still create contacts, but Amazon will be the only option for syncing.

4. Add the information for your contact. The fields are just like editing an existing contact, with the addition of a drop-down that allows you to change which account you want to sync with this contact **K**.

5. When you're finished, tap Save.

To join contacts:

1. Launch the Contacts app.

2. Find a contact that has a duplicate and tap one of them.

3. Tap Edit and then the Menu button .

4. Tap Join. A list of suggested contacts appears at the top of the Contacts list **M**.

5. Tap the duplicate contact you would like to join into this one.

6. The contacts are joined, with information from both showing as one contact **N**.

TIP Tap the Menu button on a joined contact to split it back into different contacts **O**.

L Join links two or more contacts to one.

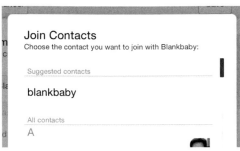

M The Fire suggests possible contacts to join.

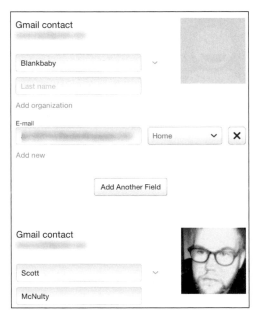

N Two contacts' worth of information in one contact entry

O Joined contacts can be split back into separate ones.

P The blue star denotes a Favorite contact.

Q Tap the Favorites tab to see only Favorite contacts.

R You can share contacts via Skype (if it is installed) and E-mail.

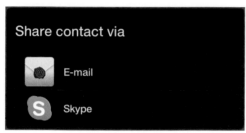

S The contact's vCard is attached to an e-mail to be shared.

To make a contact a Favorite:

1. Launch the Contacts app.

2. Find the contact you want as a Favorite and tap it.

3. Tap the star next to the contact's picture, and it will turn blue P.

4. That contact is now a Favorite. Tap the Favorites tab in the Contacts list to see only your Favorite contacts Q.

TIP To undo a Favorite, tap the contact and then the blue star, which will turn gray.

To share a contact:

1. Launch the Contacts app.

2. Tap a contact you would like to e-mail to someone.

3. Tap the Menu button and then Share.

4. The Sharing menu appears R. The options listed here will differ depending on the apps you have installed.

5. Tap E-mail to create a new e-mail with the contact attached as a vCard, a format many address programs can import easily S. Enter the e-mail address, subject, and message if you like, and then tap Send.

To change your contact sort:

1. Launch the Contacts app.

2. Tap the Menu button and tap Settings.

3. Tap Contacts General Settings. Here, you can disable backing up your contact to Amazon and determine how your contacts are sorted and displayed .

   Tap Off to turn off backup to Amazon's servers for your contacts.

   Tap Sort Order of Contact Name to set the sort to either First Last (the default) or Last, First.

   Tap Display Order of Contact Name to change how your contacts' names are displayed: First Last (the default) or Last, First.

T Contacts General Settings

Manage your Kindle Fire

Your Kindle Fire doesn't require much oversight. It does a good job of serving up content and apps and letting you surf the Web. Sometimes, though, you might need to delve into the settings or even reset to factory defaults.

Given the cloud-connected nature of your Kindle Fire, you can also change some settings on Amazon.com without ever using the Fire. This is especially handy if your Fire is lost or stolen because you can deregister the device via the website to make sure the thieves don't go on a spending spree.

In this chapter

Customizing device settings

The Fire has a dizzying array of settings that you can tweak. Most of them are app specific; they impact how you view your e-mail, for example, but not the overall experience on the device. Some settings control a general aspect of the Fire, and this section covers some of them.

To update your Kindle Fire:

1. Amazon makes improvements to the software running on your Kindle Fire from time to time. To check whether there is an update available, swipe down from the top of the device to bring up Quick Settings and tap More.

2. Tap Device.

3. Tap About A. Here, you can see some information about your Fire, including the current system version. Next to the system version is an Update Your Kindle button. When your device is up to date, that button is disabled.

4. When an update is available, tap the Update Your Kindle button, and the update is downloaded and applied. You should plug in your Kindle Fire to a power source when applying an update to ensure the update isn't interrupted by a loss of power.

> **TIP** If you don't have access to a wireless network, you can download the proper Kindle Fire update from http://www.amazon.com/gp/help/customer/display.html?nodeId=200529680. Then transfer the update using USB mode. (Connect your Fire to a computer with a mini-USB cable and copy the file over to the root of the device.)

A The current system version of your Kindle Fire. If an update available, the Update Your Kindle button will be active.

```
Your Kindle Account

Manage Your Devices

Subscription Settings

Kindle Payment Settings

Personal Document Settings

Country Settings

Manage Whispercast Membership
```

B Your Kindle Account options appear on the Manage Your Kindle site.

To change your payment type:

1. When you purchase items on your Fire, your default 1-Click payment type is used. To change which card associated with your Amazon account is used, log into http://www.amazon.com/manageyourkindle.

2. Click Kindle Payment Settings under the Your Kindle Account section **B**.

3. Your current payment method is listed **C**. Keep in mind that your Kindle uses your 1-Click payment method, so changing this setting here will also change your 1-Click setting for all of Amazon.

4. Click Edit.

continues on next page

Kindle Payment Settings

All Kindle transactions are completed with 1-Click. Changes made to your default 1-Click method will apply to future Amazon.com 1-Click transactions, but will not change your current active subscriptions.

Your Default 1-Click Payment Method

Billing Method

Edit

C Kindle Payment Settings lists the current credit card being used for any 1-Click purchases.

5. All the credit cards associated with your account are displayed 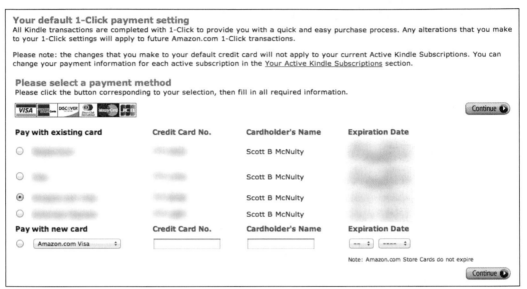. Select the one you want to use, or add a new one.

6. Click Continue. Then, select a billing address by clicking the "Use this address" button (or enter a new one).

7. Your payment method has been changed.

D Changing how you pay for things on your Kindle Fire means changing your 1-Click settings.

A Tap the Deregister button to unlink your Amazon account from your Kindle Fire.

B Before you can deregister a Kindle Fire, you have to read this warning.

Wiping and deregistering

Your Kindle Fire is tied closely to your Amazon account. If you want to sell your Kindle Fire at some point or give it to someone else in your family, it would be nice to link it to their account. In the case of selling, it might be even better to wipe it completely and restore it to the factory settings. If you were to lose your Kindle Fire, wouldn't it be great to make sure it could no longer use your account?

To deregister your Kindle Fire on the device:

1. Swipe down from the top to bring up Quick Settings and tap More.

2. Tap My Account.

3. Tap the Deregister button **A**.

4. A warning is displayed letting you know that all your content purchased from Amazon will be removed and some features of the Fire won't work **B**.

5. Tap Deregister, and the Fire is no longer registered to your account.

To reset to factory defaults:

1. Swipe down from the top to bring up Quick Settings and tap More.

2. Tap Device.

3. Tap Reset to Factory Defaults.

4. A warning displays telling you that all your content on the device will be erased and all settings reset .

5. Tap Erase Everything.

6. Upon reboot, the Kindle Fire is just like it was when it first left the factory floor.

To deregister on Amazon. com on your computer:

1. Point your browser of choice to http://www.amazon.com/manageyourkindle and log in with your Amazon account.

2. Click Manage Your Devices in the Your Kindle Account section **D**.

3. All of your Kindles are listed. Click the Deregister link next to the Kindle you want to unlink from your Amazon account **E**.

C A Factory Reset erases all the data and settings from your Fire.

> Your Kindle Account
>
> Manage Your Devices
> Subscription Settings
> Kindle Payment Settings
> Personal Document Settings
> Country Settings
> Manage Whispercast Membership

D Your Kindle Account options on the Manage Your Kindle site

E The Registered Kindles section lists all devices registered to your account.

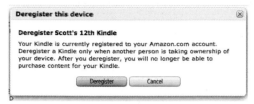

F Click Deregister to deregister your Kindle Fire remotely.

4. A warning appears letting you know that this Kindle will no longer be able to purchase content from Amazon.com **F**. Click Deregister.

5. The list of your registered Kindles reloads, and the deregistered Kindle Fire is no longer listed. The deregistered Kindle Fire no longer displays any of your Amazon content.

Index